INSIDE THE
SOVIET
EMPIRE

by the same author

The General Says No
Transit of Britain
Freedom Under Foot

INSIDE THE SOVIET EMPIRE

The Myth and the Reality

Nora Beloff

Times BOOKS

Published by TIMES BOOKS, a division of
Quadrangle/The New York Times Book Co., Inc.
Three Park Avenue, New York, N.Y. 10016

First published in Great Britain in 1979 by George Allen & Unwin, Ltd.

Library of Congress Cataloging in Publication Data

Beloff, Nora.
  Inside the Soviet empire.

  British ed. published under title:
  No travel like Russian travel.
  1. Russia – Description and travel – 1970–
2. Beloff, Nora.   I. Title.
DK29.B44 1980   914.7'04'85   79–66844
ISBN 0–8129–0878–3

Manufactured in the United States of America

Contents

Author's Preface

The journey and the book would have been impossible without the cheerful cooperation of my companion and driver, Margaret Moss. In our five weeks together, she proved an intrepid traveller, keenly aware of the funny side of things, and she enhanced the pleasures and eased the tribulations of the tour. She is the witness of the happenings I describe (some of which may be hard to believe) but is in no way responsible for the contents of the book or for its conclusions.

Two eminent writers emboldened me to add to the vast accumulation of books about the Soviet Union. The first was Edward Crankshaw, who has helped me understand the Russian empire in its historical setting. It was he who introduced me to such original Russian writers as Konstantin Paustovsky, Vladimiar Soloukhin and Vladimir Voinovich, without whose works the contemporary Soviet scene would be even harder to comprehend. The second was the late Anatoli Kuznctsov, who said 'write down everything, exactly as it happened'. This was certainly his technique in the wartime chronicle *Babi Yar*, which is essential reading before any visit to Kiev.

My special thanks to Clifford Makins, who helped filter the enormous quantity of material and impressions which I brought back from my journey; and to him and John Bright-Holmes for much-needed editorial assistance. A number of specialists kindly checked the information, though I alone must take the responsibility for errors and omissions, inevitable in dealing with such a huge subject. The spelling of Russian proper names follows the conventional British system.

The place names are in accordance with the *New Oxford Atlas* of 1975.

I am especially indebted to Victor Swoboda, Senior Lecturer in Russian and Ukrainian at the School of Slavonic Studies of the University of London. He took an enormous amount of trouble on my behalf and not only saved me from blunders but helped me to acquire additional explanatory materials.

Among the other academic personalities on whose learning and wisdom I drew were Professor Alec Nove of Glasgow, Professor Ivo Lapenna of the London School of Economics, Dr Donald Rayfield of Queen Mary College, London, and Dr Howard Spier, the Research Director at the Institute of Jewish Affairs in London.

In preparing the chapter on the Askania Nova nature reserve, I am much indebted to the Baron Edouard von Falz-Fein, nephew and heir of the founder of the reserve. He was permitted to go for much longer and see far more of it than I was, and generously allowed me to draw on his experience. Thanks also to Mrs Joanna Kilmartin, who is writing a book on European nature reserves.

I must add a special word of thanks to my friend Mrs Robin Davie, who helped me in many ways, at many times, while this book was being written.

The London staff of Intourist obligingly organised my tour and on my return answered questions, bringing the information up to date. The criticisms in the book about the Intourist Agency as a state monopoly are in no way directed against its London subsidiary. I also hope that my book may help the Soviet authorities find ways of improving the reception and care of foreign tourists: these will no doubt be contributing an increasing proportion of the Soviet Union's much-needed hard-currency revenue.

The greatest help which the Soviet authorities could give, and at no cost to themselves, would be to allow free rein to the natural hospitality of their own peoples, instead of expecting these to treat foreign guests as if they were enemy agents. All the events and conversations reported in this book took place; but, owing to the snoopiness of the Soviet administration, I have occasionally altered the names of the people and of the localities where the meetings took place.

Until President Brezhnev or his successors initiate a change of attitude, I will regretfully have to refrain from expressing my individual thanks to the many Soviet men and women, including especially the large number of students, who were kind and helpful to us during our journey. I remember them with affection.

INSIDE THE
SOVIET
EMPIRE

1

Travelling to Tbilisi

How in the world does Moscow hold its multinational empire together when the imperial splendours of London, Paris and Berlin are only fading memories? It was my nagging curiosity about the past, present and future of the Soviet empire which impelled me to tour its southern regions.

I decided to go as soon as I heard that these exotic territories, the Carpathian range, the Black Earth region, the Crimea, the Don Valley, and – most exciting of all – the famous military highway across the Caucasus, were open to privately propelled Western travellers. Most of the Soviet cities, villages and countryside are still, for foreigners, as in wartime, prohibited areas.

Along most of this itinerary, the Russians are a minority. Other races include Ukrainians, Hungarians, Poles, Jews, Georgians, Abkhazians, Kurds, Ossetians and a cross-section of the hundred-odd other ethnic communities (not to mention the innumerable cross-breeds) of which the USSR is composed. My 5,000 kilometre motoring tour took me from Chop, on the Hungarian border, south-west of the Carpathians, to Yalta in the Crimea and to Tbilisi in Georgia.

Seventeen years previously, I had travelled by car into the Soviet Union. I took the traditional Napoleonic route: Brest, Minsk, Smolensk and Moscow. I was awed by the interminable expanse of forest and plains. Distance was all.

Scenically, ethnically and climatically, this journey, in contrast to my last, promised enormous variety. While I was there temperatures rose to over 100° Fahrenheit and fell to freezing. Some regions were devastated by drought, others by flood. The route crossed two major mountain ranges, the Carpathians and the Caucasus, and many lesser hills. It spanned seven great rivers: the Dniester, the Bug, the Dnieper, the Donets, the Don, the Kuban and the Kura, and innumerable smaller streams. And it hugged the shores of the Black Sea where the scenery and the climate recalled the Mediterranean.

A few months before the tour I had spent a fortnight in Moscow. I found the top officials and academicians even more hidebound, uncommunicative and unapproachable than before. My experience increased my eagerness to penetrate into regions further away from the Kremlin.

My curiosity about the Russian imperial phenomenon probably stems from the fact that I am, at one generation removed, a member of one of its ethnic minority groups. Not that my family had anything against the Communists. My parents came from Russia in 1912, immediately after their marriage. They wanted a family and agreed that Tsarist Russia was no place for bringing it up. Their five children, of whom I was the third, were born and reared in London. Although we heard them speaking Russian to each other – especially when they did not want us to understand what they were saying – our first foreign language was French. My mother came from the St Petersburg intelligentsia and thought French culture more civilised. But she spoke excellent Russian and in later years, when members of the Soviet trade delegation visited our home in London, they congratulated her on the purity of her accent.

My father came to London as an agent from a Russian export firm. After the Revolution he stayed in the City of London and became a merchant banker in his own right, specialising in trading in chemicals with Eastern Europe. The Soviet trade delegation sent a wreath and a message of condolence to his funeral, saying that he had been the first man in the City to do business with the Russians after the Revolution.

My parental background helped me when I became Moscow correspondent of *The Observer* in the Khrushchev era. I worked there on and off – never for more than three months at a time – between 1960 and 1964. I was in the Red Square when the Russians celebrated the launching of the first spaceman, and in the Kremlin when Khrushchev announced the capture of the American pilot Gary Powers, shot down during a reconnaissance flight.

My journey to the south had a dual purpose – and I hope this account of it will appeal to a dual readership. First, it gave me the chance of visiting some of the most spectacular regions of Europe, including many I had never seen before. Secondly, it made it possible to find out how the various nationalities were faring in the present-day Soviet Union. Were they merging into the intended '*homo sovieticus*', sharing a common loyalty to Moscow, or were the communities tugging against central power? How were the people affected by the advent of the private motor car, owned by a few but dreamt of by almost everybody, giving families much greater scope for private activities? How far was the Soviet Union able to maintain its thought control against the new methods of communication: the radio, cheap travel, tapes, records, etc.? And did television help Moscow to direct opinion in the desired channels, or did it make people more aware of the hardships in their own lives?

The book is addressed, first, to potential tourists who may want to follow my trail. It is not the equivalent of an official guide, of which there are many, but may provide a traveller with background material and practical advice. Secondly it is addressed to readers who may share my curiosity about the astonishing durability of the Soviet empire but prefer to do their travelling by proxy. For me, the journey was a shattering experience and I believe I found out many things which are not widely known in the West and which throw some light on those corners of Soviet society which the Russians prefer to keep dark. I returned with the conviction that the secrecy which still blankets the Soviet Union is accounted for only partly by their fear of foreign spies. The real risk is that outsiders may observe and expose the backwardness the Soviet social and economic (though not military) apparatus.

My book retraces what I saw and what I heard: it is not a knocking operation. The Soviet regime can rightly claim that it has given the peoples under its control the longest period of peace in the whole of their turbulent history. Indeed, that point was made to me by many of the people I met during my travels. My motive was a simple one: not just to see the sights but also to meet the people.

The journey needed a lot of preparing. The first task was to recruit the right travelling companion – one who knew Russian, was willing to do all the driving, and who would be available in the month of June. I consulted the heads of Russian faculties in various British universities and it was Queen Mary College, London, that recommended Margaret Moss – Malgorzata, to use her original Polish name, and the one the Russians preferred. Margaret had come to London as an au pair girl from Warsaw, married an English school teacher and taken a BA in Russian, a qualification for which there is not at present much demand on the British labour market. When I found her she was working as a clerk for Bass Charrington Breweries while hoping to improve her prospects by getting a more advanced academic degree. With this in mind, she intended to draw on her love of animals and write a thesis on the Soviet Union's most famous nature reserve, Askania Nova.

Margaret is thirty years younger than I and was educated in communist Poland. Thus between us we spanned two generations and the two kinds of Europe. It was due to her Slavonic background, her experience of communist society and her warm, expansive personality that we were able to establish easy relations with so many of the people we met, particularly the students.

The next job was to clear the journey with the Russians, which meant going to the offices of the Intourist Travel Agency, which in 1979 celebrates its fiftieth birthday. It has the weaknesses of any monopoly. Its hotels, restaurants, service-counters, are a constant reminder of the superiority of competitive enterprise. All experienced travellers, whether they favour private or public enterprise, must surely agree that catering should be exposed to as much competition as possible. If there are two inns in a village, even supposing the landlords are both rogues, they will be trying to underprice and outbid each other. In such conditions, the client is king. In the USSR the client is a subject: he has to put up with what he gets.

I knew that the journey would be arduous and decided that I

and Margaret Moss, for whose trip I was paying, would travel *de luxe*. This cost seemed high but I was told it included the right to a car, a chauffeur and an interpreter for three hours every day. But we had our own transport and did not require an interpreter. We had to pay just the same: Intourist still lives in the old world where *de luxe* people are *expected* to require a chauffeur and a limousine.

By what seemed a curious anomaly, £21 a day was charged for each of us even though we shared our *de luxe* accommodation and services: the cost, I was told, would have been precisely the same if we had booked separately and required two rooms and two limousines. Characteristically, after years of losing money by this preposterously uneconomical method of business, Intourist woke up and, since we were there, prices have been adjusted.

Intourist now charges £48 a night for a single night (bed and *no* breakfast) and £24 per person per night, for a bed in a room for two.

Motor touring is not limited to the few who can afford these high prices. If the booking is made in time, and demand is high, most of the places along our route charge no more than from £2·50 to £4·50 a night. These are the charges for accommodation in the Intourist camps, where travellers may pitch their own tents or sleep in their own cars. Under other arrangements, beds are available under Intourist canvas or in Intourist bungalows. There are no camp sites south-west of the Carpathians or in Georgia. And there is a rigorous prohibition against spending nights outside the official designated sites.

Discrepancies are not eliminated by Intourist's custom of referring everything back to Moscow. In two of the cities, Tbilisi and Krasnodar, where we had paid for *de luxe* accommodation, the best rooms were full and we were told we must settle for 'first-class' – a Russian synonym for lower-grade. For the two days in Tbilisi, 44 roubles were refunded in cash; at the tourist exchange-rate that represented about £35. For one night at Krasnodar, I was given a chit which they said must be exchanged in London. I sent it in and received a cheque for £5.

But a tourist really worried about getting his money's

worth would be better advised to stay in the West. That is where you can get good food, polite service, a fair choice of wine, and above all good roads to permit fast but safe driving. This point was made by a Kurdish engineer (of whom more later) who was hitch-hiking across mountainous unpaved roads in Georgia: 'If you want motorways, you should have stayed at home. Perhaps in ten years we will have them. Meanwhile you should be savouring all this as part of the exotica of foreign travel.'

Intourist has another fault: its special relations with the KGB, of which we had some direct experience. A motoring tour of the Soviet Union is best enjoyed by treating it as an obstacle race – with most of the obstacles erected by Intourist. Their job is to see that tourists do not learn too much or meet too many unauthorised people. This is a less daunting proposition than it might seem, as almost all of the four-million-plus foreign tourists who visit the USSR every year go in the 'follow-my-leader' package tours. They are cheaper and much easier to control.

We applied not for press accreditation but for a regular tourist visa, though I took the precaution of informing the Soviet Embassy that I would be writing about the tour.

The cities open to foreigners and the roads along which they must travel are designated on special Intourist maps. And, just as in history books prominent personalities who have fallen out of favour become 'un-persons', so, on Intourist maps, places, however famous, can be 'un-places'. The Intourist map of the Crimea showed the peninsula without Sebastopol and I foolishly left us no time to visit this famous port. The stay at Yalta was so brief that we had to turn down an offer from a casual acquaintance to go with him by taxi to Sebastopol, where he would show us round.

Intourist had said that the bookings would take between ten days and a fortnight. I gave them a month and they took five weeks. I was in a hurry to get away partly because I had to make a detour to Munich in order to visit Radio Liberty. Aware that during my month in the Soviet Union I would be bombarded by official Party propaganda, it seemed sensible to expose myself first to a little counter-culture.

It was the dissident writer Anatoli (Tolya to his friends) Kuznetsov, then living in London, who suggested that I should go via Munich. His book *Babi Yar* is widely considered the most vivid chronicle of wartime Kiev and, as this city was to be the highlight of our journey, I had been eager to meet him. A censored version of Kuznetsov's book originally appeared in Moscow, where it is now out of print and banned. Later it came out in an unexpurgated form in London. The Soviet censor had deleted all references damaging to the Communist Party, the Red Army and the partisans. In the London edition the censored paragraphs were printed in bold type.

After Kuznetsov's defection, the Soviet authorities took their revenge by blackening his character. His old mother, now living alone, half blind, in a Kiev suburb, heard the rumour that her only son had disgraced himself and committed suicide. She had learnt he was alive but he thought she might be reassured if I called to tell her that her Tolya was well and happy. I put a letter from Kuznetsov to his mother in my bag and said I would deliver it if I found this could be done without antagonising the Soviet bureaucracy.

At the Munich headquarters of Radio Liberty I met a lively bunch of men (very few women) who had come from all parts of the USSR. They were as querulous and factious as most exiles. Outwardly cheerful, they must still have found it painful to be living so close to their own country with so little prospect of returning. The Soviet authorities treated them as a menace, tarred them with abusive propaganda and jammed their broadcasts. Radio Liberty is inaudible in many of the places we visited, but we were told of one occasion when a group of university teachers at Rostov heard the station by mistake; they were twiddling the knob and found they were listening to such a pure and literary Russian that they guessed it could not be the BBC or the Voice of America even before they heard the signal *Svoboda* (Russian for freedom). Sometime the broadcasts even reach Siberia. In his book *To Build a Castle*, Vladimir Bukovsky says Radio Liberty could be heard in his labour camp on a powerful radio set made by a convict-technician from spare parts assembled in his place of work.

In Munich I got a first glimpse of the ethnic tensions between the non-Russian minorities in the regions which I would be visiting. The Georgians were enraged by a broadcast from Radio Moscow, of which they gave me a text, which announced that the 'autonomous' province of Abkhazia, at present an integral part of the Georgian 'Republic', wanted to quit Georgia and merge with the Russian 'Federal Republic'. Moscow announced that the matter was under review. As everyone at Radio Liberty knew, Georgia is only nominally a republic, and in reality is an integral part of the highly unitary USSR. But the Georgians, to a man, felt this was a plot to deprive Georgia of its rightful frontiers. Abkhazia was on my route and I kept the text of the Moscow broadcast, hoping to find out what the Abkhazians thought.

From Munich I flew to Vienna, where Pepsi-Cola have their European headquarters. Pepsi's remarkable success in the Soviet Union had been widely recognised in the international business community and I had written to the Corporation's Chairman, Mr Donald Kendall, declaring my interest. 'There is no question that the Pepsi-Cola story in the Soviet Union is one that should be told,' Kendall had replied. 'I think it demonstrates a new way of life in the Soviet Union.' His staff in Vienna gave me a letter of introduction to the Pepsi bottling plant at Novorossiysk.

Apart from my fascination with the 'Pepsi-colonisation' of the USSR (see Chapter 13), I was also seeking an excuse to visit a Russian factory. The bottling plant, though set up by the Americans, was at present under exclusively Soviet management. Scheduled visits to preselected plants are notoriously unrevealing. In his recently published reminiscences, Leonid Brezhnev recalls his post-war experience in Zaporozhye, when he always made a point of visiting factories unannounced. 'I would not go where I'd been invited, where perhaps even the roads were swept clean. ...' The communists were not the first Russians to put on a show. In the eighteenth century, when the Empress Catherine went on a royal progress, her minister Potemkin had the façades of villages set up, complete with happy peasants, to reassure her that her people appreciated her benevolent despotism. Before accepting invitations to a 'typical' Soviet factory, all visiting Western trade unionists should remember Potemkin.

I had arranged to meet Margaret Moss in Vienna. To my horror, the evening before we were due to leave she turned up having lost her voice, and as white as a sheet. My better self urged me to take her home. But we agreed to soldier on. After the journey was over, she confessed that her condition might have been psychosomatic. Her first enthusiasm for the trip had been followed by panic. She had told the girls in her office that she hoped she would fall ill and be unable to go.

Her recovery was remarkable. Only four days later she spent twelve hours driving in sweltering heat on appalling roads, and then, after taking a bath and changing into her long cotton dress, still summoned up the energy to go dancing.

But knowing nothing of her recuperative powers I spent an uneasy night before we set off to the Avis Vienna office to pick up our rented Volkswagen. I had wanted a small car and all the experts I consulted agreed that the Volkswagen was the sturdiest little model available. Avis provided us with a brand-new biscuit-coloured car, which wherever we went was a focus of interest and attraction. It certainly had faults: the quarterlight windows did not open; there were no mud-flaps; and the excessively tight seat belts left no choice but a squeezed stomach or the risk of a fatal accident. But the car survived the appalling roads without ever giving us a moment's trouble. Though it was new when we collected it, I had no idea of the internal condition of its engine when we gave it back. Had I known the road conditions, I would have taken a jeep rather than a mini-vehicle. Avis had been told of our route but never warned us about the conditions. I was pleased it was their car and not mine.

From Vienna, we drove straight to Budapest. On the once-beautiful banks of the Danube there were smelly and solid traffic jams for several miles. The Budapest Hilton, built with panache within the walls of an ancient Hungarian palace, provided opulence and comfort as great as any other luxury hotel on the international circuit. We decided that Hungary qualified as an honorary member of the Western world, for Budapest was certainly no preparation or half-way house to what was in store for us as we crossed the Latoritsa River, entered Chop, and embarked on our Soviet Odyssey.

2
Entrance Through Chop

The frontier post on our way out of Hungary into the Soviet Union was little more than a shack. Its corrugated roof reminded me of a wartime Anderson air-raid shelter.

The customs official gave our luggage a cursory glance but we had to wait an hour for his attention. There were several uniformed Hungarians around but only one on duty. As he opened the boot of the car, I was wondering whether to take the advice of an experienced Western businessman and slip him a bribe. The decision was taken out of my hands: he helped himself to a packet of Player's cigarettes.

We grinned goodbye and drove a few hundred metres to the much larger and apparently brand-new Soviet post. Mock marbled flooring, potted plants, spacious round glass tables and a shiny new coffee bar. There was no coffee, as the water-heating machine had broken down. While we were waiting a group of men came in for a snack. Could they have sausages and bread? Sausages yes, but there was no bread. 'What do you expect us to eat the sausages with, pastry?'

An unsmiling young soldier indicated where we should place the car and the laborious task of examining everything we had brought in began at once. The operation immobilised a large team of men and women for several hours. Mechanics took the car apart, investigating every cranny in which documents and treasures could be concealed; two men and a translator leafed through all the written material; a man counted our money and inspected our travellers' cheques; another went through our personal belongings, unscrewing bottles and opening tubes. A female medical inspector in a dazzling white overall scrutinised our fruit.

On our way through Austria we had bought some oranges and apples. I refused to believe Margaret's warning that we would be forbidden to take them into the Soviet Union. Could it be true, as tourists allege, that the Russian officials prohibit the import of fresh food so that they can themselves eat commodities unavailable on the Soviet market? Not so, according to a voluble and highly articulate English-speaking Intourist official who welcomed us on arrival. Soviet crops, he said, had been cruelly blighted by bacteria imported in alien food. Certainly, if it was a charade, the lady doctor was a good actress. She gave special attention to one particular orange, cutting a little black spot on the peel, placing this in a polythene bag and treating it as a rare scientific specimen. The rest of the orange she handed to Margaret and told her to eat it forthwith as it could not possibly be allowed into the Soviet Union. We finally managed to come away, neither of us remember how, with two oranges and three apples rolling around on the back seat. They were very refreshing in the hot and dusty regions further on.

But although we were permitted to eat our fruit on the spot (presumably importing the deadly germs in our digestive tracts) the suspicion lingered on that the ban on imports is imposed for the benefit of local officials. The Russians themselves may be unaware how this procedure enrages foreign visitors. One Polish family coming back from a holiday in Bulgaria with their car full of fresh fruit – melons, peaches, apricots, plums – threw them all on the road and ground them into the dust rather than allow the Russians to regale themselves at Polish expense.

In my previous visits to the USSR, my bags and books had been checked but this was the first time they took my handbag. After a long delay the bag was returned with all its contents but they had had time enough to read Tolya's letter to his mother, Mrs Kuznetsov.

The documents they confiscated were not in the least confidential. First, an analysis of Soviet trade with West

European countries based on official statistics and compiled by Philip Hanson of Birmingham University. It had been given to me in Vienna and I had thrown it into the car, knowing I would be too busy to read it until after the tour. Second, the script of the Moscow broadcast about the Abkhazia autonomous region which I had picked up in Munich. Third, articles written for the London magazine *The Banker* and for the New York quarterly *Foreign Policy* on the East European Comecon bloc. Our Intourist guide, with whom I chatted, knew all about my visit to Moscow earlier that year. Yes, he had heard that I had been sponsored by *The Banker* – did the magazine not belong to the *Financial Times* group? I congratulated him on being better informed than most of my readers.

But surely the authorities did not believe that my analysis of the obstacles to Comecon integration would provoke riots and disturbances? No, he said, but the police have their own rules: the articles would be restored on my way out. I never saw them again but by that time I had other things on my mind. I had brought them in because I was going to seven university towns: Lvov, Kiev, Kharkov, Zaporozhye, Yalta, Krasnodar and Tbilisi, and hoped to meet academics who might be interested in the subject and willing to discuss my conclusions.

While I was arguing with the Intourist man, Margaret was making friends with the young mechanics who were taking the Volkswagen apart. Neither she nor they could find a fan belt nor knew whether there was supposed to be one. Having unscrewed the machine, would they be able to put it together again? Yes, they would guarantee it. And if the engine would not start? They would work on it until it did.

The Russians (although we were now in the Ukrainian Soviet Republic, the frontier officals spoke Russian to each other as well as to us) asked Margaret why she had left Poland. When they heard she was married, they expressed astonishment that her husband had allowed her to come. They were the first of many people we met during our travels who could not conceive of a wife as an independent partner, leading her own life.

The inspection of our possessions was suddenly interrupted when a Hungarian customs official rushed into the Soviet frontier post as if he were about to seek political asylum. It turned out that in helping himself to our cigarettes he had forgotten the formality of taking away our transit visas. We were consequently officially still in Hungary. Luckily for him we had not thrown away our little pink slips. He snatched them from us and strode back to his own country.

When the check-up was finished, the Intourist people arranged for us to change some money at the tourist rate of 1·27 roubles for £1. It was Humpty-Dumpty who told Alice that he used words to mean what he wanted them to mean. The Soviet Government feels that way about its currency. Money has nothing to do with value and anyone with any sense does as much business as possible by barter (you give me a ticket to the opera and I'll give you a shampoo and set). In these circumstances, it is difficult to admit any ethical objection (although there can be severe legal penalties) for finding non-monetary means of payment. A traveller has to remember that to acquire the number of roubles he could get for selling one pair of Levi jeans he would have to part with 150 hard-earned pounds. We parted with the pounds. Most tourists, very sensibly, do not.

The zany nature of the multiple exchange rate was brought home to us when we noticed that in a hard-currency store we could buy some delicious Russian nut chocolate for 33 American cents. The same item was being sold to the Russians for 1·40 roubles – which at the tourist exchange rate is almost six times as much.

After getting our money, we went to procure our petrol supply. We spent only £65 for 130 ten-litre coupons, though since then the price has been raised both for foreigners and for Soviet citizens and looks like continuing to rise. Residents as well as foreign visitors use coupons rather than cash and most Soviet petrol stations have no cash register. This saves time and trouble and eliminates the risk of robberies.

We filled up and set out. The road had an unfinished, dusty surface suggesting a wide country lane. We drove north for 23 kilometres along flat country to the quiet little town of Uzhgorod where we spent our first night. It was the main town in the trans-Carpathian province which, between the wars, had belonged to Czechoslovakia: the Soviet Union annexed it in July 1945. The official justification was that the region should belong to the Ukraine as most of the population is Ukrainian. Whether they wanted to be ruled from Moscow is another question.

Certainly during the last war, after the German retreat, the Russians had a lot of trouble reasserting Moscow's control over the Ukraine. In his memoirs, Khrushchev describes the situation in the West Ukraine when he left the region and was called back to Moscow in 1946: 'It happened in the midst of our struggle against the Ukrainian nationalists. The Carpathian Mountains were literally out of bounds (i.e. no-go areas) for us, because from behind every bush, from behind every tree, at every turn of the road, a government official was in danger of a terrorist attack.' Resistance was suppressed by 1950 though sporadic acts of terrorism went on until 1952.

Western historians generally agree that the ethnic factor was only the excuse for the annexation of additional territory: the real reason was geopolitical and strategic. Stalin wanted to assert a Soviet presence in the Danube regions. The extension of Moscow's rule, for the first time in Russia's history, to the other side of the mountains may also have appealed to Stalin's imperial pride. He was one up on the Tsars.

The Intourist hotel at Uzhgorod managed to look both new and dilapidated. A very large and severe woman with gleaming gold teeth was waiting for us at the reception desk. She told us that if we wanted anything, the Intourist office would be open the next morning at nine. That was one and a half hours after we were scheduled to leave.

Our *de luxe* suite had two good-sized rooms, a bathroom, a hall and, like most Intourist Hotels, no room service. The walls were cracked, the furniture rickety and the bathroom fittings looked decidedly pre-war. The impression that we were moving into the past was reinforced by the period suit, waistcoat and watch-chain worn by Lenin, who was depicted in black against a red background on a mural covering a wall of a six-storey building, which confronted us as we went out on to our balcony.

It was the American writer Lincoln Steffens who, returning from the Soviet Union in the fervent post-revolutionary days, pronounced the famous dictum: 'I have been over into the future and it works.' Today, a returning visitor might say: 'I have been over into the past and it creaks.' The more adventurous Soviet young now look West to know what is new, radical, daring, and feel that under the dead hand of the Communist theocracy, their country has become a backwater. The stolid conservativism of Soviet society as shown in their behaviour, style of living, and artistic and architectural tastes, was one of the dominant impressions that stayed with me throughout the journey. But I should add, of course, that I never got anywhere near the military-industrial complex: judging by results, it is as advanced as, and in some aspects more advanced than, any in the world.

One of the trials of Intourist travelling is that the only place where you can eat in the evening is the hotel restaurant which always has an ear-bursting dance band. Before going in, we went for a quiet walk. We wandered round wide, dual-carriage way roads with hardly any traffic and saw empty shop windows, giving an eerie feeling of an abandoned city. Though it is thirty-four years since the Soviet Union annexed the sub-Carpathian province of which Uzhgorod is capital, the region still seems unassimilated. This may be partly because, as we discovered the following day, there are still no proper roads to its Soviet hinterland.

Ideologically, the local Party officials have evidently done what they can to integrate the new territories. We had our first exposure to the inescapable Party posters, steel emblems nailed on lamp-posts, stone statues, photographs of party dignitaries, and announcements of the Party's economic achievements. It was like being at the climax of an election campaign but with no prospects of a polling-day.

Back in the restaurant the band was playing a compromise between Negro jazz and Russian schmaltz. Most of the clientele were middle-aged, wearing dark suits or cotton dresses. The dance-floor was crammed with large bodies which seemed to be going up and down in a kind of hippopotamus jig.

A well-dressed, good-looking man lurched up to our table and invited Margaret to dance. She remembered seeing him propped up against the wall outside the hotel as we arrived. He had followed us into the hotel and, while I was registering at reception, he was trying to get Margaret to talk. Having asked where she was from, he said he wanted to hear more about England. She replied 'Perhaps, later.' His eyes were bloodshot and his speech slurred. Even before she saw that he was drunk, Margaret had taken an instant dislike to him. Only later did we discover that he was a police agent.

A plump young man, who looked like a traditional Russian peasant, presented us with a printed menu. There were twenty-five pages, listing succulent dishes – soups, fish, meat, salads, desserts, pastries, fruit – with exotic and exciting names. A very few of the items were followed by the prices added in ink – which meant that they are sometimes available. The night we were there, the only choice was what the waiter called 'beefsteak', which turned out to be a meat loaf consisting of a small amount of unidentifiable meat mixed with a lot of bread. The menu was signed by the three people responsible – the manager, the chief cook and the accountant. The date of its publication, in small letters on the back, was June 1965.

At the end of the meal the waiter brought us some lukewarm tea. Could we have it hot? The answer was no. Once again, the water-heating machine had broken down. After all the tension and worry of the day this was too much: we laughed till it hurt.

Although our watches showed it was only 10 p.m. and we had been told that the restaurant stayed open until 12, the staff were plainly impatient to get rid of us. Evidently they deliberately adjusted the clock to minimise their hours of work. Although the region has been part of the Soviet Union for thirty-three years, people still think and talk in Czech time. By the official Moscow time (the Moskovskoye, as they call it), it is two hours later: we put forward our clocks to midnight. Breakfast, as the reception desk had told us, would be served from seven o'clock. We had no wish to stay any longer at Uzhgorod and, as we faced a hard mountain drive, along reputedly difficult roads, we decided to eat as soon as the restaurant opened and make an early start.

The next morning, when our readjusted watches said seven o'clock Moskovskoye, we were packed, dressed and ready to go. We found the hotel dead to the world and the woman looking after the car park said nothing would open for two hours. The seven had been the Czech time by which the local people still lived and we had got up at 5 a.m. It was pointless to wait so long for breakfast. We had brought tea bags with us and all we needed was hot water.

3
Breakfast in the Carpathians

Our first full day in the Soviet Union could hardly have started better. The road was wide, in excellent condition, and there was almost no traffic. The scenery as we began to climb was beautiful and benign: not craggy, snowbound peaks like the Alps but rolling hills. The silence was broken only by the sound of water. After about a quarter of an hour we came to a brightly painted and cheerful looking roadhouse – a tourist attraction fairly typical of central Europe. It was too early for business, and the shutters were drawn. Could we wake up the residents and ask for boiling water? Margaret stayed in the car while I toured the premises shouting and throwing pebbles at the windows. There was no response. We drove off wondering what time the place opened. We wrongly presumed that we would find similar facilities dotted along our route. On the contrary, inns and eating-places are extremely rare along Soviet main roads and Soviet highways, and the closed café near Uzhgorod was brighter and newer than anything else we saw.

The climb was through largely uninhabited country and we drove for an hour without seeing a house. Then we came to what looked like a quarry with a couple of factories and, a few hundred metres farther on, a lane leading to a clump of cottages. By now we were beginning to yearn for breakfast. We turned off the main road and this time I stayed in the car while Margaret, equipped with chewing-gum and cigarettes, went out to see if these could be exchanged for hot water and, if possible, for fresh bread. The car was soon surrounded by village children who looked ragged and, though certainly not hungry, victims of a poor diet. Chewing-gum was the only thing they begged for.

We had about ten packets of Wrigley's – and if readers are thinking of following our route I would advise them to take at least fifty. Our supply ran out very early in the tour and after that we embarrassingly often had to say 'Nyet'. I was particularly conscious of failing to observe the spirit of détente when, on our way home, we drove by a squad of young soldiers repairing the road and had to ignore their friendly waves and shouts for *zhvachka* – Russian slang for chewing-gum.

The children were delighted by the car and wanted to know where it and I, in that order, came from. They said they supposed the 'A' (representing Austria) stood for 'Anglia'. I asked if any of them were learning English. They replied no, they were taught German at school.

Meanwhile, Margaret had gone down the lane and met a woman pushing a bicycle. Seeing that Margaret was a foreigner she immediately asked her whether she had anything to sell, particularly children's clothes. Margaret said no but offered cigarettes and asked for hot water. The woman took her back to her cottage. It was Sunday and her husband was still in bed. After whispering a word to him she suggested that, instead of taking the water away, we should both come to the cottage and have a proper breakfast. While Margaret walked back to fetch me, the man got up and dressed. Soon we were ushered into their very clean and well kept home. Apart from a small kitchen, where the wife was preparing the meal, they had one room of about twelve feet square. It housed him and her, his mother and one obstreperous little girl, also partial to chewing-gum.

The relationship with the family, which had begun on a material basis, now became warm and cheerful. The welcome was genuine even though they knew that, apart from a few cigarettes, we had nothing to offer. The spread for such an obviously un-affluent family was embarrassingly generous. Fresh eggs were cooked and smoked sausage, cheeses and pickles were laid out; slices of freshly baked bread were cut, and generously smeared with fresh butter. Our host, whose wife introduced him as Vasya, proposed some vodka. Margaret smiled demurely and replied that she never drank while driving. I do not normally lace my breakfast with alcohol, but asked for 'just a little drop' to liven up the atmosphere. I had supposed there was vodka in their cupboard and I was embarrassed when I saw him leaving the house. I begged his wife to go after him and tell him I did not want him to buy vodka on our account and had only accepted the offer because I had assumed they might have a little at home. 'Oh, we have! We make our own but it's too crude for visitors so he's gone to buy some better stuff from the shop.'

Granny had been on the point of taking the little girl to church but she was easily persuaded to join in the feast. She and the child spoke a language which I did not understand. Were they speaking Czech? Margaret asked, having studied a little of that language in college. The old lady looked wistful and Margaret thought she was close to tears. But her son intervened, ruled out any talk about Czechoslovakia, and told us the language was a sub-Carpathian dialect. Margaret still believes it was Czech.

We drank toasts to our friendship and to world peace and expressed proper appreciation for the breakfast. I told them I was a writer and Margaret said she worked in a brewery. We then asked them what they did. Vasya had a job in the nearby tool factory but said the installations were 'very primitive'. His wife worked in a sewing-shop, making suits and dresses. Given two relatively skilled workers, I was surprised that they did not have more than a one-roomed cottage for four. The most conspicuous item of furniture was a huge, old-fashioned wireless set, which they said no longer worked. They also had a small garden; but Granny complained that the rain had ruined the tomatoes and there would be no fresh vegetables. The whole of the southern part of the USSR had had an excessively wet summer and wherever we travelled tomatoes were a luxury. Usually, the only available salad was cucumber served with sour cream and chopped onions: an excellent dish, but not one to be repeated too often.

Just as we were getting more friendly and relaxed, a villager rapped on the door and said the militia were asking about the car. As I went out to see what they wanted I heard Vasya's wife muttering 'The bastards!' The police were standing by the car and their first question was 'Who do you know in this village?' I told them about our hot-water mission and our trouble in finding refreshment along the road. They denied my right to take the car off the scheduled route – though we were only a few metres up the lane. Finally, after I had shown them our passports, vouchers and Intourist correspondence, they stopped hectoring and wished us a happy journey. By the time we were leaving, the whole village had gathered. Vasya and his wife, who had followed us back to the car, were glowering at the police, but looked more angry than frightened.

Is it right to accept invitations to private homes in the Soviet Union, knowing that it may be the inmates and not the casual caller who takes the rap? This was a question I had often asked myself during previous visits. In his perceptive reminiscences, *The Kremlin and the Embassy*, Sir William Hayter, former British Ambassador to Moscow, recalled that during the several years he had served as junior diplomat in Moscow in the 1930s he had only once had an unscheduled chat with local people. This happened during a walk in Georgia, when some workmen came up and asked whether things were better in Britain than in the Soviet Union. On receiving an affirmative answer, they said that that was just what they supposed. Sir William noted: 'I record this trivial incident only because it was practically the sole occasion during these years on which I had a really frank conversation with a Russian.'

Things are different now and on my visits to the Soviet Union I had many 'really frank conversations' with Russians, though always with a slight foreboding about the consequences. None the less, my meeting with Vasya did not change my view that if adult Soviet citizens wish to receive outsiders it would be insulting to refuse their hospitality. The danger is incomparably less than in the 1930s, when a joke about Stalin could be a capital offence. In these more civilised times, the penalty is more likely to be a loss of some special privilege: permission to travel abroad, job promotion, favours in the allocation of housing or cars. Vasya's proletarian family had nothing to lose. As we drove on, we speculated about how the militia had found us: had they followed us all the way from Uzhgorod or did they happen to notice a foreign car by the road? Or had they been tipped off by the villagers, perhaps one of the children, who wanted to be in the Party's good books?

Suddenly the road petered out. We were still high in the mountains and found ourselves bumping along a narrow and rocky dirt track. Then, coming down to Mukachevo, about fifty kilometres from Uzhgorod, four roads merged and we began to have traffic problems. There were still hardly any private cars, but the dust raised by the trucks and military vehicles produced that ancient London phenomenon, a pea-soup fog.

In this early phase of our journey Margaret, who later confessed that she had only been driving for three years, was extremely cautious. She gave way to anything on wheels, even tractors, if they wanted to pass. As the route wound down the mountain, Soviet lorry drivers swerved around and ahead of us. We crawled along, inhaling the black smoke from their low-grade fuel.

At one point our Volkswagen went over a big rock, making a crunching noise which suggested that our engine was being ground into scrap.

Margaret had panicked before leaving London. Now panic caught up with me in the eastern foothills of the Carpathians, before we had completed the first hundred kilometres of our tour. We had slowed down to 20, 15, 10 and now 5 kilometres an hour: and had another 4,900 kilometres to go. The dust and dirt churned up by the passing vehicles obscured the countryside. Several members of my family had said I was crazy to come: perhaps they were right.

We pulled up at the roadside and inspected the car, which, amazingly had stayed intact. Margaret, who was sheet-white and had not yet recovered her voice, lit a cigarette. She never smoked inside the car but I always agreed to stop when she needed nicotine. On most occasions I was glad of a swig or a nibble but this was no time for refreshment. 'Let's do a U-turn and go home,' I heard myself say. In the past, as a news reporter, I had persevered through far more hair-raising experiences. But this was supposed to be a jaunt; I was travelling on my own behalf and there was nothing to prevent me from scrapping the expedition before Margaret or the Volkswagen – or both – collapsed and it all ended in ridicule and disaster.

If we had turned back, I could surely have reclaimed the £1,650 I had paid in advance for *de luxe* accommodation for two people for one month. Our itinerary had been drawn up in accordance with the official Intourist map and the roads on which we travelled were marked with thick red lines, denoting, according to the key, 'motor road', 'autoroute' or 'autobahn'. We would rarely be travelling more than 450 kilometres a day, which on Western standards is not very much. We could at least argue that Intourist had sold us vouchers for a motoring holiday which, through no fault of their own, they could not deliver.

Had Margaret's panic coincided with mine, we would have cancelled the trip. But I only learnt about hers after we got home: by the time my nerve was shaking (luckily it never cracked) she had recovered and would not hear of going back. We set off again, in the middle of the road: driving on the right is compulsory in the Soviet Union, as elsewhere on the European continent, but on these roads it was quite impossible.

Watching the endless trek of military and civilian lorries, I was astonished to see how many of them were carrying or towing other vehicles which had evidently been unable to take the battering. It seemed amazing that the Soviet Union, which plans its economy so far ahead, should have allowed the huge increase in the manufacture and import of motor vehicles without first ensuring an adequate road network.

The war historian Liddell Hart wrote that it was the lack of paved roads that prevented the German motorised divisions, in 1941, from getting to Moscow by Christmas, as had been planned. Perhaps Soviet policy makers have a mental block against making it too easy to drive into their country. But, from the economic and social points of view, something has gone seriously wrong. There is certainly a case, often stridently argued in the West, for 'homes before roads'. No one has ever argued the case for vehicles before roads.

No city has suffered as much from this inverted policy as

Stryy, which lies in the eastern foothills of the mountains and serves as a major traffic junction. When we were there the roads were not yet paved. It took us half an hour to go half a mile through its winding streets. And the air was so thick with fumes and dust that, even though we were stuck for a long time in the central square, we could hardly see the regulation Lenin statue on the lawn. Towering over the town, in letters which stretched over several buildings, we just managed to make out the proclamation: 'Glory to the Communist Party!'

In the final fifty kilometres to Lvov, the road improved. For some stretches, new paving had been laid and the track widened into a multi-lane, dual-carriage, Western-type motorway. But tourists should look out: there are rarely any indications on Soviet highways to show when the road will narrow. We often found ourselves speeding along on what appeared still to be a dual carriageway and then being suddenly confronted with traffic coming directly at us.

As we came close to Lvov, and later to Kiev, we saw that the roads into these cities were being massively enlarged and improved. Apparently this was part of the Soviet Union's great sprucing up in preparation for the 1980 Olympic Games. Lvov had been selected for the handball trials.

We reached our Lvov hotel along wide, smooth roads in the late afternoon. But the day's driving ordeal was not yet over.

4
To Russia with Lvov

Soviet streets are often named after doctrinally blessed events. The Intourist Hotel (in Polish times the George) stands at the junction of two roads now known as 'Lvov's seven hundred years' (commemorating the city's foundation) and 'May the First'. After a harrowing day's drive, we were relieved to see the road conveniently widen in front of the hotel. We pulled up, but no sooner had I got out than Margaret was ordered to move along. The hotel, she was told, must be approached by an elusive one-way side road. She set off, got lost, and took another quarter of an hour to reach a spot just 200 metres beyond where she had started. Nor was this all: after we had unloaded our things, we were told to park the car in another part of the town.

By this time even Margaret was testy. The head porter sullenly agreed to direct her there, but refused to come back on foot. So she drove to the parking-place, then took the porter back to the hotel, then drove out again and then walked back. The second time round, a middle-aged Russian named Volodya approached her to say that he knew the city very well and would be happy to show us round. He arranged to meet us at 6.30, by the Lenin statue.

When we came back through Lvov at the end of our journey the police themselves exposed the futility of this extra driving: several cars were already parked in the front driveway, causing no obstruction at all, and we were told to leave ours with the rest.

Margaret and I had one argument which we never resolved. She believed that packets of cigarettes or pairs of tights should be handed out only as a reward for services rendered. I took the soft line, believing that, in the Soviet Union, nothing will come of nothing and tips should be used as inducements. This was the issue on which we came nearest to quarrelling. Her arguments were moral. I was older, more cynical – and also more reluctant than she was to trundle our own luggage and do our own chores.

Our hotel suite was of majestic, pre-Communist proportions. The colour TV worked; the two bedside lamps did not. As in all Soviet hotels, there was a woman sitting at a desk on each floor, looking after the keys and keeping an eye on the clients. They are called *dezhournaya* after the French *du jour*, though they sit all through the night as well as all the day. Margaret, bearing no gifts, went to ask if we could have refreshments brought to our room. She came back in fits of laughter. 'We never serve food in the rooms', she had been told, 'except if it is ordered by nobility.' The woman used the German word *Graf*, count, but obviously referred to any titled person. Margaret's father had been a land-owner, mine a merchant banker; neither of us qualified for the aristocracy.

After a rest we went down to the lobby and talked to the staff about the appalling state of the roads. But did we not know how much the Soviet Union had suffered during the war? Houses were the first necessity. It would have been tactless to point out that Germany also had been shattered and now had roads as well as homes.

At the newspaper stand I asked for one of the two main national dailies, *Pravda* or *Izvestia*. The woman in charge said she received only eleven or twelve copies of each of these and they had been sold out long ago. She was offended when I turned down her offer of the *Morning Star*. 'It comes from your own country,' she said, 'and just because it's Communist you won't read it.' If it had not been Communist, it would not have been there: for the English-speaking visitor it was the *Morning Star* or nothing.

It was not only in Lvov but everywhere we went that the official Party papers were in short supply. This is just one of the consequences of shortage of paper and pulp. Timber is needed to earn hard currency. Although the Soviet Union is well endowed with forests, wood cutting is under-mechanised and old-fashioned. Moscow is constantly picking on the timber industry as even guiltier than others of 'under-fulfilling' the annual plan.

Further, newspapers are very cheap and can, of course, be used for other things besides reading. Later in our journey a couple of obliging young men showed us round an open market-place and offered to buy us some cherries. These were being sold, at three roubles a kilo, by a row of plump peasant women, each sitting in front of her own bucket-load. The tourist rate was 1·27 roubles for £1 sterling while we were there, but on the free market the pound was selling for 7 roubles, so the price of the cherries was not extortionate. One of the women weighed out 2 kilos but was about to throw them back into the basket when she saw we had nothing to put them in. It was a sellers' market. One of our escorts sprinted across the market-place, bought that day's *Pravda* (price 3 kopecks, 0·03 roubles), twisted its six pages into a cornet-shape, and in went the cherries.

Books as well as newspapers are both cheap and in short supply. A distinguished Soviet Academician recently surprised his scientific hosts in London when he asked them where he could buy the Russian original of Turgenev's short stories. No, they were not banned in Moscow; they were compulsory reading at his daughter's school, but totally unobtainable.

While I was at the hotel news-stand, a seedy, bespectacled man shuffled up and asked if we happened to have *Playboy* or any other 'sexy' magazines. The woman at the counter shooed him away. When we went out, he was still hovering and hoping.

Libertarian literature is in high demand – partly, perhaps, because the permissive society and its works are anathema to the Communist Party. A small number of Western best-sellers are occasionally translated and published in very limited editions: they go off the market overnight and are more frequently obtained by Soviet citizens through unauthorised channels. I heard of one amply proportioned Ukrainian matron, married to a diplomat, who when returning from a term of office in New Delhi carried, packed in her bra, not only Orwell's *Animal Farm* but also Harold Robbins's much thicker *The Carpetbaggers*. Even had we been so minded,

Margaret and I were the wrong shape for this form of contraband.

Our rendezvous with Volodya being at 6.30, we went to eat at a time which in the West would have fallen between lunch and dinner. But the Russians often eat late in the afternoon (indeed in some of the Intourist hotels no soup is served in any meal taken after 6.30 p.m., even though you could have hors d'œuvres, meat and dessert).

We arrived on time for Volodya and, at 7, just as we were giving him up, he arrived, red-faced and breathless. We were treated to a long lament about the unreliability of his wife and daughter. They had been told to wake him up after his siesta, in time to prepare for our meeting, and now he had dishonoured himself by keeping such esteemed ladies waiting.

Volodya then proceeded to take us not on a tour but on an anti-tour: his object was to show us the city at its worst. His animosity to the regime was so pronounced that at first I suspected he might be an *agent provocateur*. But he did not appear to have any ulterior motive at all: far from provoking indiscretions or illegal transactions, he did not even listen to what we had to say. All he wanted was a sympathetic outlet for his pent-up frustrations.

We started by going to the Communist Party headquarters. Outside were the customary glass-encased photographs of members of the Party who had especially distinguished themselves. 'Lenin would have shot the lot,' said Volodya. 'They use their power to feather their own nests.' I asked him if by 'they' he meant the local Communist leaders or the national Politburo (the small caucus which governs the country)? 'Both,' he replied. According to him, the rot started with Stalin. 'But would Stalin have been possible without Lenin?' I asked. As he saw it, Lenin was pure and selfless, and the absolute power he bequeathed to his successors was misused to enrich themselves and their children.

Volodya asserted that the Party potentates lived in palaces while the rest of the people were crowded into hovels. I asked him where these palaces were, and if we could see them. He said they were outside the city and their location was kept secret. Were Volodya's allegations true? I remembered an account given to me by an American businessman who, in the heyday of détente, had been invited to the country home of a senior Party man. All you could see from the road was a wooden fence, a courtyard and straggling poultry, but inside was a magnificent marble-pillared establishment, worthy of any American tycoon. Alexander Yanov, a journalist who defected from the Soviet Union in 1974, said that super luxury was confined to the Party's top thousand. On the only occasion he visited one of them he passed through an ordinary-looking gate and was dazzled by the magnificence of the interior. The installations included a swimming pool, and Western *avant-garde* furnishing and decoration. According to Article 13 of the Brezhnev 1977 constitution, 'The personal property of citizens and the right to inherit it are protected by the State.' There are no death duties.

Volodya next took us to the Roman Catholic church in the heart of Lvov, which was packed for evening service. The worshippers belonged to the Polish minority who remained inside the Soviet Union after the war. Most of the three million who lived in the lands which Stalin annexed had volunteered to return to Poland in exchange for Ukrainians who had been living in Poland. The minority who remained are stolidly refusing to be de-Christianised, even though it is harder to preserve religious customs in the Soviet Union than it is in modern Poland. Since 1964, courses in atheism are compulsory in all Soviet schools and colleges.

The remaining Poles also cling to their own language. A Pole in charge of a petrol station outside Lvov, where we stopped to refill, insisted on giving Polish answers to questions asked in Russian. In another Ukrainian city, Margaret met a Polish woman who said she was a university graduate and earned her living looking after the parking lot. She was convinced that her ethnic origins had prevented her from making her way in life. In 1939, when she was one year old, her father, then doing his military service in the Red Army, was shot – along with all other Poles in his unit. Stalin must have known that once he had agreed with Hitler on another partition of Poland he could hardly count on the loyalty of Polish soldiers when the Red Army was needed to police the Soviet share of their country.

The second church we visited was a massive ruin. It stood in the centre of a large graveyard; the windows were broken and pieces of masonry were falling down. It had once served as a barn but now seemed totally deserted.

We reached it by trolley-bus, travelling free. Normally on Soviet buses and trams you buy tickets and stamp them yourself in the machine placed inside the bus. We had no tickets but this was Sunday, there were no inspectors around, and Volodya told us not to worry. Even he could not complain about the public transport. It was very good everywhere we went.

He took us down some dilapidated streets and insisted that we accompany him into the worker's cafeteria – *stolovaya*, as it is called – to sample the badness of the food. It was a depressingly dirty place and all the customers were male. He bought one portion of some greasy little dumplings with an unidentifiable stuffing. I agreed they were repulsive but Margaret later confessed to me that she found them rather tasty.

Then to a large bakery (all shops in the Soviet Union are state-owned) where we used the forks, chained to the wall, to poke the bread and test its freshness. We bought a little, which seemed just edible, for our next day's picnic. Volodya claimed that the authorities did not mind how much stale bread was left over as it was recycled into the next day's supply. Then a tour of four or five shoe-shops, all selling identically ugly styles at identical prices. Volodya said one pair would cost him a week's work. He accused 'them' of encouraging simple people to make extravagant purchases as a spur to work harder. What sounded to us a sensible form of economic incentive was for Volodya just one more piece of evidence that the Party was exploiting the people.

Another grievance was the commission shop (in which the supplier of the goods gets part of the profits). These exist all over the Soviet Union and usually deal in second-hand valuables: samovars, jewels, embroideries and other family heirlooms. Some sell foreign goods. Soviet citizens are now allowed to receive individual parcels from friends and relatives abroad. Many otherwise destitute people live on the proceeds.

But in Lvov, according to Volodya, there was a commission shop selling fresh food. In most Soviet cities, food is sold either in state shops or in the open market-place. In Lvov, he said, all the fresh stuff – meat, poultry, fish – went to this special retailer and nothing was obtainable in the ordinary shops at the fixed prices, which people like himself could afford to pay.

Volodya told us something about his life and times. He was not a wage earner but a craftsman employed when his services were needed. A good deal of his work was connected with the schools and as these were on holiday he was earning less than his usual 150 roubles. He said that it was very difficult to make ends meet and that he never saved anything. His daughter could not forgive him for failing to produce the 2,000 roubles required to secure admission to a university. (Lvov has a great cultural tradition. Even before the Soviets took over, the city boasted of a university, founded in 1661; a polytechnic, 1844; a veterinary institution, 1879; and a music conservatoire, 1904.) Volodya said that he was teaching his daughter his own trade and that she would have to follow in his footsteps. It seems to be a common practice for ambitious parents in the Soviet Union to pay the admission authorities to take their offspring. One Intourist guide in another Ukrainian city confirmed that 2,000 roubles is a fairly usual sum. An outstandingly brilliant student, or someone with good Party connections, can be admitted without baksheesh but in most cases there is a fixed tariff. This varies according to location and faculty. The medical school, which releases students from the drudgery of two or three years as a private in the Red Army, can cost as much as 5,000 roubles in Kiev and 12,000 in Baku, capital of the Azerbaijan Republic. A Jew is said to have been told that, before emigrating, he would have to pay back to the state the 5,000 roubles which had been spent on his education. He suggested settling for 2,000 as he had paid 3,000 already.

Despite his disgruntlement, Volodya was not doing too badly. Air transport is plentiful and fares are far cheaper in the Soviet Union than in the West (perhaps because it is militarily useful to have large numbers of transport aircraft available in case of crisis). He was proposing to fly out to the Black Sea the following month, to spend his holidays with his mother, who lived near Sochi. We said we would be getting there before him and he sat down on a park bench and wrote her a greetings letter, which he asked us to deliver. Unfortunately we did not have time to stop.

Like most Russians we met during our tour, Volodya declined to come into the Intourist hotel. As we parted at the Lenin statue, he kissed my hand as though there had never been a revolution.

But I must not be unfair to Lvov: it is a spacious city, with well tended parks and gardens, and most of its citizens look well fed and well shod. There are bad cases: old men earning a few pennies by weighing passers-by on ancient machines; old ladies selling bunches of flowers tied up in straw. But conspicuous poverty, though greater than in Moscow or Kiev, is the exception rather than the rule.

Lvov was built by Ukrainians in the thirteenth century to protect Galicia against the Tartar-Mongol raids and, considering its violent history, it is fortunate to have preserved so many of its historic buildings. In the present century alone Lvov has belonged to four different territorial entities. Until 1918 it was in the crown-lands of the Austro-Hungarian Empire. Between the two world wars it was part of Poland. It was allocated to the Soviet Union in 1939, under the Molotov-Ribbentrop pact (the record of which is deleted from Polish and Soviet history books). After the pact, Stalin went to the point of organising a plebiscite to show that annexation was what the people wanted. According to one man who was in Lvov at the end of 1939, when the polling took place, the only choice was to vote in favour: voting was compulsory and there was no secret ballot. The Germans conquered Lvov in 1941 and were driven out in 1944. Since then it has been the capital of an *oblast* (Russian administrative unit) within the Ukrainian Republic of the USSR.

But, though many ancient buildings are still standing, the descendants of the builders have vanished. Before the Soviet conquest, Lvov was inhabited mainly by Poles, Jews and Germans (who call it Lemberg). During the last war the inhabitants were massacred or dispersed and replaced by Ukrainians and Russians. The new population has not yet developed a corporate identity. Lvov has changed hands so often that it does not seem to belong to anyone – and no one feels that he belongs to Lvov.

5
Kiev : The Pity and the Glory

We did the 550 kilometres from Lvov to Kiev in a single day. As a special concession (or perhaps they never noticed it), Intourist waived the regulation 500 kilometre daily maximum imposed on motoring tourists. But it was a sweltering journey, the roads were cluttered, bumpy and ill paved and it took twelve hours of almost non-stop driving. We never passed a single inn or café along the route. And in the end I began to think that, in some things, Intourist knows best.

Indeed, I might have done better to refer back to that great traveller's guidebook published by Karl Baedeker in 1914, which has 40 maps and 78 plans and which as indicated on its title page has a fairly comprehensive coverage: 'Russia, with Teheran, Port Arthur and Peking'. Reprinted, in its original form, in 1971, it still offers a useful service. The orthodox Communist line is that everything up-to-date began with the Red Revolution. Baedeker fills in the historical gap, indicating how much was already there. It permits a more realistic perception of subsequent transformations. Its special section, 'Motoring and cycling' (today, foreign visitors may not cycle), should have put me on my guard. It said the highways from Moscow to the big cities were in excellent condition for motorists but lesser roads 'are of a very different character': they still are.

The road went through the fertile Black Earth region, which stretches from the Carpathians all the way to Mongolia. It has served as the granary of Russia since the seventeenth century, when, as the Intourist booklet says: 'the outstanding Ukrainian statesman and general, Bogdan Khmelnitsky (of whom we saw many statues) liberated the Ukraine from the Polish-Lithuanian feudal yoke'. What they do not say is that he called in the Russians to support him against the Poles and that within the next hundred years the Ukraine was gradually absorbed into the Russian empire.

The Black Earth region, according to the 1914 *Baedeker*, 'is one of the most important sources of the world's corn market'. The Russians still exercise a big impact on the world corn market, but as importers not exporters. For though they led the world in the Red Revolution they have been remarkably laggard with the 'green revolution' – that is the application of new methods which enable farm workers and farmland to multiply output ten or twenty times.

Modernisation is a slow business and the climate is unhelpful. But the progress will doubtless be helped by the proliferation of trucks which made our journey so uncomfortable. For in the past the big collectives have generally lived in virtual isolation from each other, depending for everything on their own resources. Improved transport facilities now permit them to specialise and so make much better use of chemicals and machinery. Back in March, 1977, however, Brezhnev warned farm managers not to jump the gun. He said that once they heard the news that meat would be available from specialised meat producers they all promptly eliminated their own livestock: 'This is the only explanation for the alarming fact that in recent years a considerable number of collective and state farms have discontinued breeding pigs and poultry. (Fortunately individual workers are allowed to keep a few animals of their own.) A steady supply of meat for the population has not yet been achieved and this situation cannot be tolerated. ...' He *has* tolerated it.

Our journey taught us all we needed to know about Soviet trucks: the shape of their behinds, the noise of the engines, the smell of the black low-grade exhaust fumes. But from the road, it was difficult to see what was going on inside the collectives. The farms are separated from the main road either by neatly fenced cottages (the Ukrainians are tidier than the Russians; they paint their houses and decorate their bus-stops with elaborate mosaics) or by rows of trees, with bands of white insecticide round their trunks; also by hedges and barbed wire. From the glimpses of activities on the fields agricultural work still seems to depend more on womanpower than on machines. We caught sight of long rows of peasant-women stooping over their work both in the blazing midday sun, and in pelting rain.

The few metres between the road and the farmland are frequently used as pasture for privately owned cattle. Peasants tend a small herd of their own – sometimes just one man or woman to one cow. In some areas, the roadside is planted with sunflowers, beans, maize, often with streams and ditches running through them. After rain (and we had a lot on the way home), the roadside turns into mud – inaccessible if you are wearing sandals.

Frequently we had to drive for an hour or two before we could find a suitable stopping place. Picnics were a useful device for attracting the locals. Once we found a shady bank and some workmen parked their truck and came to join us. They asked the usual questions about our car's speed, cost and origin. We offered them a smoke and talked about jobs, pay and food in our respective countries.

The truck driver, evidently the team leader, said he was earning 200 roubles a month (a university lecturer starts at 125 roubles). The most disgruntled, and perhaps the least sober, of the group said that he came from Leningrad but would not say what took him away. He complained that he earned a pitiful 70 or 80 roubles a month, not enough to keep a family. Then the driver interrupted this down-to-earth chatter and asked 'What do you think of the neutron bomb?' (the American weapon which destroys people but not buildings or vehicles). It seemed no use telling him that I thought it a reasonable response to the great leap in Soviet nuclear power represented by the installation of the SS20 missiles in Eastern Europe. Instead I asked him what he thought. Presumably the team leader was a Party member and would be attending compulsory lectures. Throughout our stay, the neutron bomb was the biggest international issue. His reply was curiously noncommital: 'I believe people should live in peace and stop trying to destroy each other.' His Leningrad mate was sceptical: 'I expect that they (meaning us) don't know any more about the bomb than we do.'

We stopped on the way at an all-purpose village shop to stock up. It had no fresh fruit, meat, or vegetables and the bread supply had run out: we bought butter and sweet buns. Then Margaret went back to see if payment in kind might produce better results. The woman asked for clothes, but we had nothing to offer. Two Woolworth lipsticks were exchanged for a 2-litre flagon of fresh apple juice, which, by that time, was just what we needed.

We arrived late, cross and crumpled. Luckily we found our way to the right hotel. On our return journey, when we came back to the Lybid Hotel, we were told we had to go on to the Dniepro. Tourists are never told in advance where they are to be staying. In many of the towns we and the Intourist staff spent a lot of time trying to find out where we were supposed to be.

The city of Kiev more than justified the miseries of the drive. Its site, on the hills overlooking the Dnieper river, is magnificent and the buildings a triumph of traditional town-planning. The river bank and the whole of the island within the river bend are covered in park, woodland and orchard. The wide boulevards are divided by carefully tended gardens, with unvandalised shrubberies, flower-beds and lawns.

Kiev suffered heavy war damage. Just before the Germans arrived, the Soviet police placed time bombs under the main buildings of the Kreshchatik – Kiev's equivalent of Piccadilly or the Champs Elysées – and also under the thousand-year-old Cathedral of the Assumption, in the Pechersk-Lavra complex of monastic and other religious buildings. This is something the Intourist guide glosses over. According to the official version, it was the Germans, or Fascists, as the Russians prefer to call them, who were responsible for all the destruction, and it is this tale which has been retold by countless travellers returning to the West. Yet it is not true. The series of huge explosions which wrecked the Kreshchatik, and the whole centre of the city, took place several days after the Germans were installed. The first building to go up in flames was the

German military headquarters and many Germans were killed or badly injured. As a Ukrainian-born British university lecturer commented, 'The Nazis were sadists, but no one suggests they were masochists!'

The destruction of the great cathedral took place a few days later; once again, the Soviet secret police had left time-bombs. According to Anatoli Kuznetsov, a few days before the Germans arrived the people living in the area had seen the security police temporarily cordoning off the entire area and had witnessed the arrival and departure of several trucks before the grounds were reopened.

When the Germans made their triumphal entry into the city they had the monastery bells of the Lavra ring out their victory and the German command sternly repressed any looting by German soldiers of the historic treasures belonging to its churches and chapels. They then set up gun emplacements on the hill within the Lavra compound and had considerable difficulty rescuing German weapons when the explosions began. The fire lasted for several days and destroyed archives and monuments, and the Russians listed the conflagrations among the German war crimes.

This is, of course, not to defend the Wehrmacht's record in Kiev. On their way out, three years later, the Germans did as much damage as they could during their hurried retreat.

Kiev, known in the old days as 'the city of a thousand churches', now has twenty, of which only three operate. These include the vast Cathedral of St Vladimir, built between 1862 and 1896 by Beretti and Berhandt, in neo-Byzantine style. One Russian, whose family fled the Revolution when he was only six, made his first return to Kiev in the autumn of 1978 and I heard him reporting on his visit in the crypt of the Orthodox Church of White Russians in the Rue du Tsarévitch at Nice. He said he had been particularly moved by the size and ardour of the Kiev congregation and had observed at the St Vladimir Cathedral a soldier in Red Army uniform who took a candle and openly participated in the ceremony.

The Cathedral of St Sophia, built in the eleventh and reconstructed in the seventeenth century, which has one central and fourteen smaller golden domes, is the finest and most spectacular of the buildings still standing. Inside, we were told, there were fine mosaics and frescoes, but, as we arrived on the keeper's rest day, we never saw them. One of the best views of Kiev is from the eighteenth century Baroque church of St Andrew's, designed by the Italian architect Rastrelli. It has white domes and gilded doors and stands on the Andreyevski hill, from which, says the Intourist guide, the Apostle Andrew first preached the gospel to the Slavs.

Despite the destruction of the great cathedral, Kiev is still dominated by the surviving group of buildings in the Pechersk-Lavra monastic complex, once Russia's most revered religious institution. The surviving monuments include the medieval gateway, the massive bell tower, several smaller chapels and the dormitories and refectories of the old monastery. At first the monks lived in caves in the hill. Underground catacombs can still be visited. But later the religious brotherhood moved into the very lavish premises and our Intourist guide mocked men who preached self-sacrifice while living so well. Could the same not be said of Communist leaders? I asked. She laughed and replied, 'only the elite ...' She must herself have been a Party member, but would hardly qualify for high living.

One of the old monastic buildings has been transformed into a museum of historical jewellery with a dazzling display of pre-400 BC. Scythian gold. This was the biggest attraction at Lavra and the lobby was packed with disciplined groups waiting to go in. Foreigners travelling individually were allowed to jump the queue. The ornaments were large, intricate and deserved detailed inspection, and I had a stand-up row with an old lady keeper who objected to our loitering. She demanded that we attach ourselves to a large group of visiting Russians who were progressing at the regulation pace. I refused to be herded and later regretted having reduced her to tears.

There were two war memorials in Kiev, which had nothing to do with one another, but, to me, respectively represented the glory and the pity of war.

The first is a gigantic granite column standing behind the tomb of the Unknown Soldier, in the well-groomed Park of Eternal Glory. On a tiled platform in front of the obelisk, groups of little girls were parading for fifteen minutes at a time. They wore white organdy ribbons in their hair, navy blue skirts and khaki blouses buttoned to the chin. Goose-stepping rhythmically up and down, they were as unflinchingly solemn as the Grenadier Guards.

All this was part of a national effort, started in 1975, the thirtieth anniversary of the victory over 'the Nazis' (the enemy is never referred to as Germany), to revive military ardour. The cult of military glory is central to Soviet education. New generations are taught that victory over the Nazis was the finest page in Soviet history and urged, not too successfully, to lead austere lives, to despise consumerism (*veshchism* – thing-ism, as it is called) and revere war veterans.*

The pity of war is commemorated at Babi Yar, where some 60,000 or 80,000 people were massacred, including the whole of Kiev's Jewish community. The site is in a northern suburb of the city; the memorial is a bronze sculpture of more human dimension, set in a grove of newly planted trees. The killing was done by Germans, with manual aid from resident Ukrainians: some had welcomed the Germans against the Russians; others had no choice but to kill or be killed.

The blight of anti-Semitism still hangs over Kiev. When Edward Crankshaw visited the town in 1957, soon after it was reopened to foreigners, he asked to be taken to Babi Yar. At first, his well turned-out Kiev-born guide pretended he had never heard of the place. When Crankshaw insisted, the man asked 'Why do you want to go and see a lot of dead Jews? There are far too many here still alive ...'

In the 1960s, during Khrushchev's more liberal era, Yevgeny Yevtushenko was allowed to publish his famous poem about Babi Yar. It opens with the words 'No monument

---

* When we reached Zaporozhye, the war memorial took the form of a stone female, built on the scale of an Egyptian pyramid, carrying a wreath. 'Laurels for peace?' I asked the guide. 'No, oak leaves for invincibility.'

Later, at the smaller town of Krasnodar, the parading children were of both sexes and carried real – although, I was assured, unloaded – rifles. A boy and girl, in joint command, stood on raised pedestals on either side of the monument. As I went up to read the inscription to fallen warriors, the girl stepped down and asked me, 'Comrade, are those spectacles medicated?' They were tinted; if they had just been showy sunglasses I would have been asked to take them off. The girl had no prescriptive right to enforce her order: just moral suasion.

stands over Babi Yar' – but this is no longer true. What is significant however is that the plaque at its foot is dedicated to 'the victims of Fascist crimes', with no mention of the fact that most of them were Jews.

Babi Yar is still not part of the scheduled Intourist trip. But the guides today are more sophisticated than in 1957 and are polite and helpful to those foreigners who wish to go. Families and friends of the victims still leave bunches of wild flowers around the pedestal of the monument. These are in striking – and perhaps deliberate – contrast to the elaborate wreaths ritually laid at the Park of Glory.

The most astonishing piece of official information we were given about Kiev was on its post-war expansion. The planners had allowed for a population of one million. Now, partly as a result of the incorporation of outlying hamlets into the sprawling mass, the number is 2,320,000. Of these 75 per cent are Ukrainian, 10 per cent Jewish and only 8 per cent Russian. Yet in official business – whether military or civilian – Russian is the normal language.

The failure to check the city's growth is hardly surprising. The Soviet Union has strict laws requiring town dwellers to carry identity cards (the Russians call them internal 'passports', but this is misleading, as they do not entitle holders to travel abroad). Peasants working on the collective farms have no identity papers and without them are tied to the land on which they work. But there are many ways of eluding the regulations and the Soviet Union has been no more successful than other developing countries in preventing the exodus from the countryside into the towns.

What, to me, was most strange was that after the wartime slaughter so many Jews wanted to come, or, having escaped from the enemy, wanted to come back to Kiev. Today the Jews all crowd into the big cities where they have a chance to live together and to enjoy greater cultural opportunities. In the old days, before the Nazi massacres, there were whole regions of the countryside populated by Jews. Today there are no more Jewish villages – and no more fiddlers on the roof.

Statistics on ethnic identity must be treated with caution. Hardly anyone we met belonged exclusively to one nationality. Nor is this anything new: Konstantin Paustovsky, born in 1892, one of the greatest Russian twentieth-century writers, was a glittering and successful example of racial mix. One of his grandfathers was a Don Cossack who brought back a Turkish captive wife from the wars; another was a Ukrainian public notary, who married a pious Catholic Pole.

Yet, even allowing for interracial cross-breeding, Kiev is predominantly Ukrainian, whereas its language is predominantly Russian. This is much less true of the Ukrainian countryside, but in the capital Russian is used in the ubiquitous Party posters, in official announcements, and in almost all university courses.

In her new book *L'Empire éclaté*, Hélène Carrère d'Encausse demonstrates that Russification in the Ukraine is deliberate policy. Citing unofficial figures at the time of the last Soviet census (no figures on this sensitive subject are public), she notes that the number of schools using the Ukrainian language has declined in the last twenty years from 28,000 to 23,000. The 5,000-odd Russian-language schools tend to be in the big towns and at higher educational levels. But in the Ukraine, and in all other non-Russian parts of the 'Soviet Union', the principal agent of Russification, as she says, is the Red Army.

The predominance of the Russian language reflects a political reality. The Ukraine and the fourteen other Soviet 'republics' are no more than administrative units in the highly centralised Soviet Union ruled from Moscow. They have no more independence than a French *préfecture*. But in Moscow-controlled territories the mighty arm of the central authority is not the prefect but the Party Secretary. All executive power, says the 1914 *Baedeker*, is 'vested in the autocratic Tsar'. The power has now been taken over by the Communist Party's Politburo, which is, nationally and linguistically, predominantly Russian. No manifestations of nationalism are allowed today any more than they were in Tsarist times.

The divergence between the notion of a Ukrainian 'republic', bolstered by separate representation at the United Nations, and the reality of Moscow rule makes Soviet officials in the Ukraine particularly touchy about President Carter's human rights campaign. Soviet–American relations in the summer of 1978 were bad in Moscow but even worse at Kiev.

Since 1973 the Americans have had a Consul at Kiev in exchange for allowing a Soviet Consulate in New York. The staff of five are constantly trailed and live in a state of total isolation, under a thick cloud of hostility and distrust. 'They behave to us as if we were Satan', said the wife of one of the staff. The Consulate looks after official delegations, businessmen, technicians, cultural and scientific emissaries and an endless stream of US tourists, many of whom come to the Soviet Union in search of family roots.

About 800 Soviet citizens visit the Consulate each year, seeking visas to emigrate under the family reunion clause of the 1973 Helsinki Agreement. But it is the Soviet authorities who finally decide who may leave. No Ukrainians who wish to stay in the Soviet Union would dare be seen entering the US premises except on Soviet Government business.

I had a letter of introduction to the Consul and I asked him whether he thought it wise to call on the families of dissidents? If I did, he said, I would never be allowed back into the Soviet Union. This was the reason why, regretfully, I decided that I could not visit Anatoli Kuznetsov's mother.

But, whether they like it or not, foreign tourists are a magnet to the disaffected and during our brief stay in Kiev we spent much of our time in their company. Margaret was now making her own friends. A handsome, bearded Georgian spent hours with her, pouring out his woes, saying he had no future in this corrupt and unhappy country and telling her how he longed – unavailingly and despairingly – to go West. Another escort took her on a drive which went well beyond the scheduled Intourist excursion. He was a Party man with a good job and had a flashy Soviet car, with seats covered in goatskin. They went upriver to an ancient monastery, now being restored but still closed to the general public. Then, back in Kiev, they visited the former Jewish quarter of Podol and saw a small whitewashed building which was Kiev's only operating synagogue. The cobbled, twisted streets of Podol are now slum-land and Margaret was warned it was dangerous to go there alone at night.

The purpose of the drive, as Margaret discovered, was to ask her if she could find a Polish girl willing to marry a Russian. He explained that he was acting on behalf of a friend who was willing to pay for a formal match as he believed that once he got into Poland to join a wife it might be easier to cross to the West.

While I was on my own, I was approached by a couple of well-dressed boys of eighteen or nineteen who offered to show me round. The one who did all the talking said they had finished school but that life was so futile that it was hardly worth going on to college. I asked why he did not go to Siberia, where many young people were helping develop the new resources. 'I will never go to Siberia except as a prisoner,' he replied. The boy showed off his knowledge of the recent writings of dissidents and said he had an uncle in West Germany who kept him informed.

The boys and I went down the Kreshchatik and sat in the park. The more articulate of the two said his only hope would be to marry a Jewish girl and apply to emigrate. Then a woman in dark glasses sat down at the end of our bench; the talker got up and said she was probably an informer so we all walked away. The boys said that they would like to meet Margaret and we arranged to meet the next afternoon. They never turned up.

But while we were waiting for them we were approached by a female black marketeer, with a shining row of gold teeth, who wanted to buy clothes or currency. She said the police had raided her flat and, though they had not prosecuted her, they had helped themselves to one thousand roubles' worth of her stuff. She would have to start refurbishing her stock all over again. Apart from seeking sympathy for her plight, she wondered whether we could find a Westerner willing to marry her. We told her we had nothing to sell and not much hope of hooking her a husband. Hers was the third request for a suitable spouse. We thought we might stay in Kiev and set up a marriage bureau.

We left with a lingering sense of guilt: we had failed to convey words of comfort to Kuznetsov's mother. Was it true, as I was later assured by a graduate of Kiev University, that I could have had the letter passed on while I was in Kiev with no difficulty at all? All I had to do was to address myself to any young man who wore his hair over his ears – in other words who was not a die-hard communist. The graduate who gave us this startling information was working at Kharkov, which was our next stopping place. But he told us not to worry as he was visiting Kiev himself the following month and would deliver the letter while he was there. And so he did.

6

Kharkov : A Piano for a Samovar

It was in the lobby of the Lybid Hotel, just after 7 a.m. We were about to set out on the 478-kilometre drive to Kharkov and I was seeking sympathy and help not for myself but for an American who had just received the news from home that his grandson had died. Having heard him speak English in the restaurant the night I arrived, I asked him whether he had any connection with the American Consul. He said no, he was in Kiev attending a conference on chemical engineering. He did not know there was a consul. Later, I discovered that the Consulate, cordoned off from local life, did not know there was a conference.

The night before we left, however, a member of the Consulate was looking for the American delegate to deliver the message of bereavement, which had come via the US Embassy in Moscow. He was asked to return home at once.

The next morning the American was in the lobby trying to explain that he wanted an immediate booking back to Boston. I helped him to tell the hotel staff what had happened but nobody seemed to care. Transport had been laid on for the tourists two hours later and there would be no cars available before then. The doorman told the American he should try to pick up a taxi from the rank, a few hundred metres down the road. The woman in charge of travel said she did not know whether there were early planes to Warsaw, Moscow, or any other city from which he could fly west. And she made it clear she had no intention of troubling to find out. He took out his wallet and showed the hotel staff, mostly female, photos of the two-year-old grandchild he had lost. Their sullen indifference, as far as one could tell, was not anti-American. They were resigned to the brutishness of life. 'Human beings die like flies,' said one of them shrugging her shoulders.

After this gloomy start the drive, once again through the flat Black Earth region, seemed monotonous and interminable. I have never seen so many fruit trees – or eaten so little fresh fruit. Shops in the towns and villages had no fresh fruit and, apart from cabbages, no fresh vegetables. But we did buy a bag of cherries from women at the roadside. They were selling the produce of their private gardens and their main concern was with bulk sales for jam making. As the cherries were very ripe, we persuaded them to allow us to buy no more than we could digest.

From the Intourist pamphlet one might suppose that the Kharkov region was industrialised only after the 1917 Revolution. But the 1914 *Baedeker* notes that it was already 'the administrative centre of the great iron industry and coal mines of South Russia'. Kharkov is the city from which the Bolsheviks declared the creation of the Ukrainian Soviet Socialist Republic in 1917. Kiev went on resisting until 1921 and it was not pardoned and reinstated as the capital of the Ukraine until 1934.

Kharkov changed hands six times during the German invasion and very little of historical or architectural interest has been left standing. It was by necessity rather than choice that our one-month tour included three visits to the city. I wanted to visit the Crimea as well as Georgia and had assumed that it would be possible to drive from one to the other along the north coast of the Black Sea. According to the Soviet motoring atlas of 1977, which we bought later at a bookshop in Krasnodar, there are several roads near the sea. But these are closed to foreign tourists. Intourist arranged for us to go to Kharkov, then south to Yalta, then all the way back again, then south-east to Tbilisi; nor was there any way of avoiding a third visit to Kharkov on our way home. The Soviet security mania added 500 kilometres to our journey.

'Why on earth didn't you take a boat from Yalta to Sochi?'

we were asked by a couple of cheerful young Russians who had parked their car and joined us during one of our picnic stops. They had asked if we had anything to sell. When they heard we had nothing they stayed on anyway, for a chat. They were wearing white T-shirts stamped with pop Polish slogans and said they travelled all the time as they were 'photo-reporters' – an activity they refused to define, except to say that it had nothing to do with newspapers.

They assured us that in summertime there were many boats touring the Black Sea resorts. At our next stop we consulted the Intourist office. But, as I guessed, everything would have had to be referred back to Moscow and it was far too late to make the changes.

On my return to London I asked Intourist whether foreigners were allowed to take this sea route. It seems that they may, but places are scarce as very few of the boats take cars.

Kharkov manages to conceal the ugliness of its new buildings and the absence of its old ones behind an abundance of trees and greenery. But while we were there the whole city was disrupted by the extension of the underground metro. The detours and one-way signs were driving the locals as well as visitors to distraction.

In retrospect, our entry into Kharkov was farcical though, at the time, we were not amused. On the way in, a man behind us, queueing for petrol, got out of a battered Zaporozhets (a poorer version of the Beetle) and asked for a light. When he saw Margaret's English lighter, he offered to buy it for 10 roubles. We got talking and told him we were worried about our tyres. Avis had not warned us that there are no gauges and pressure pumps at Soviet petrol stations. The man said he kept a gauge in his car and we were welcome to use it. After filling up we drove off together and stopped by the roadside to take advantage of his offer (it turned out to be unnecessary: the tyres retained constant pressure right through the journey). We did not know how close we were to Kharkov, nor had we any idea of the chaotic state of its road system. When the man offered to lead us to the Intourist hotel, Margaret said our car was more powerful than his, and we would probably get to Kharkov first.

She obviously touched a raw nerve. We got into our respective cars, the Zaporozhets gave out an enormous roar, and he disappeared in a cloud of dust. We chugged along as usual and further on we saw him waiting for us. Soon we were following him through Kharkov's back streets, unpaved little lanes, probably not much changed since the 1914 *Baedeker* days.

A red light held us up and we lost him again. We supposed he must have turned off. Margaret did a U-turn and we found ourselves going in the wrong direction down a one-way street, confronted by a large fleet of honking lorries. In the subsequent havoc, an old hag stuck her head through the open window on my side and shouted that foreigners who do not know how to drive should keep out of 'our country'.

Later we retrieved our guide and drove at a comfortable ten metres behind him. Suddenly flames burst from his car. We stopped. He got out, pulled a burning rag out of the boot and threw it on the pavement, stamped on it and jumped back into his seat. He then led us safely to our destination. But his pride had been hurt and he drove off without even saying goodbye.

The 1914 *Baedeker* provides the addresses of two places in Kharkov where English visitors could feel at home: the British Vice-Consulate and the English Club, which had the rather un-English name 'Helfferich-Ladet Sporting Club'.

Though the West has no longer any residential representatives, Kharkov is still an international centre. It has played a leading part in Soviet scientific and particularly nuclear development (the Intourist guide boasts that Kharkov scientists split the atom in 1932 and that Kharkov is the only Soviet city producing turbines for atomic power stations). It attracts many researchers and students from other European communist countries and from Asia, Africa, the Middle East and Latin America.

In Moscow, there is a separate university for blacks, named Lumumba, after the murdered Congolese leader. But in the provincial universities the blacks attend the Soviet Institutes and in Kharkov, which specialises in engineering, there is a substantial contingent of black students.

It was in Kharkov that I met two of them from Chad, who

were discussing reports of a cease-fire between the French-backed government and the left-wing rebels. I expressed the hope that their country would be spared the horrors of a civil war. But they were going back the following week precisely to try to rekindle the revolutionary flame and prevent what they saw as a patched-up peace with their country's neocolonial exploiters. Not all Third World students embrace the missionary dogma, but the Soviets are doing their best to spread the message.

The more affluent members of the international and multi-ethnic community spend a good deal of their time at the Intourist hotel, built before the Revolution, which provides the best food and pop music in town. When we were there a new motel was about to be opened and other motorists may hope to be spared Margaret's parking ordeal. The woman at the parking lot said that foreigners were forbidden to keep their cars in the yard – she unlocked a garage for the Volkswagen that had a deep pit in the middle, apparently for the use of mechanics working on large lorries. The wheels of our little car could only just span the hole. Margaret thought that at any moment she and the car would fall in. She was still trembling when she came back to our room.

When leaving, we distributed a few cigarettes to some men who were sitting around the yard doing nothing in particular (of whom there were many wherever we went) and they pushed the car out by hand. And on our subsequent visits to Kharkov we refused to have our car treated differently from Soviet ones. Anyone who travels in the Soviet Union should know how to say 'Nyet'.

Our suite had the space and height common to the pre-1917 hotels and, as in all other Intourist establishments, the curtains were too narrow to cover the windows. Did the management *always* get the measurements wrong? The locals I consulted thought it more likely that the right lengths of fabric were delivered but some of the material found its way into private homes.

We had an entrance hall, a cloakroom, bedroom, bathroom and sitting-room. We were also provided with a colour TV, a monumental fridge and an upright piano. We asked for a cup of tea but there was no water on our floor and it had to be ordered from the restaurant. We waited one and a half hours for two glasses – of tea (cups are for coffee). By that time we were getting light-headed and devised a plan to lug the piano to the nearest market-place and barter it for an old-fashioned samovar (the new ones depend on electric plugs), which would enable us to have tea on tap.

When we went down for dinner, all the tables were occupied and we were seated with a young married couple – an athletic-looking East German husband and a pretty, blonde Ukrainian wife. They had met at Kharkov University and were about to leave for East Berlin, where he had a job waiting for him at the Ministry of Finance.

In addition to his regular studies, he said, he had spent two months working on the Baikal-Amur Magistral Railway (BAM, as the Russians call it). This second trans-Siberian line will open up territories rich in oil and other minerals and is vital to Russia's future. But the climate limits work to summer months and Komsomol youth, students and prisoners provide indispensable extra manpower. The German said that students are not allowed to meet the prisoners, who work on different sections of the track, but everyone knows that prison labour is used. Those who go voluntarily are very well paid but are physically and politically severely vetted. I met a Polish engineer graduate who said that he and his friends had applied and all had been turned down. The work is tough and the hours long but, for Eastern Europeans, the financial incentives are enormous. The German came back with 900 roubles. During the same time the girl, then his fiancée, earned 50 roubles picking fruit in the Crimea.

The last war still dominates Soviet films, fiction and art, and having seen the official efforts to keep its memory alive I asked the couple whether this propaganda did not strain relations between the Soviet people and the Germans. Not at all, they said. Many Russian girls were eager to marry German husbands and only too pleased to live in East Germany, where life is so much easier. The coupling was sometimes the other way round. At Rostov, I had long discussions with a remarkably intelligent graduate student named Genya, who had married a German girl and also opted for East Germany. Genya had an Armenian father, a Russian mother, was born in Tashkent, schooled in Leningrad, and was leaving Rostov the following week to settle down with his wife in Leipzig. First he would have to learn German. He did not even know the language of his future country but had no compunction about changing nationality and – at least legally – about becoming a German.

At Kharkov again, Margaret's dancing served as a magnet. One of the Middle-Eastern students joined our table and asked whether we would like to meet a young friend, Lova, who worked for the Komsomol. Lova declined to come into the hotel and we met him at a café nearby. He told us later that he had previously been reprimanded by his Party chief for fraternising with West German visitors. He deeply resented the complaint and remained on excellent terms with the Germans, whom he hoped to see that summer at Helsinki.

Apart from his regular work, Lova, who was twenty-seven, spent a lot of time on voluntary social work: arranging holidays, excursions and exhibitions, as well as helping young people who were in any kind of trouble. His wife Natasha travelled widely, working as propagandist for the Party. He was a fully paid up Communist and I asked him whether this meant being a Marxist. No, he said, Karl Marx was a great teacher who had advanced our understanding of social history. But how could nineteenth-century philosophers be expected to solve the practical problems of today? Yet Lova certainly thought of himself as a socialist. He expressed moral disapproval of 'the acquisitive society' and was appalled at the idea that in the West young people coming out of school or college often found it impossible to get jobs.

Lova was sufficiently well informed to know that, with welfare benefits, the unemployed in the West lived better than the average Soviet wage earner. But he was passionately convinced it was society's collective responsibility to provide the individual with education, health, decent surroundings and economic security. Personally he thought Scandinavian social democracy would suit him best.

One evening we went to his flat, where Natasha served us home-baked cakes and tea. Lova told us that he was especially interested in psychology and in the relationship between the printed word and the mind's absorptive capacity. He asked us to send him any good Western books on the subject. He also wanted Solzhenitsyn's *August 1914*, a fictionalised account of the behaviour of the Russians at the beginning of the First World War. Though the book has never been published in the Soviet Union, its existence is well known through the underground samizdat and Western broadcasts.

After some discussion, he and Natasha agreed that, if we could get the volumes as far as Budapest, they or their friends would pick them up during the coming summer holidays. East-European customs officials rarely read Russian and the Russian frontier police hardly ever trouble to search Soviet delegations travelling inside the Communist bloc.

While Lova and Natasha were discussing these arrangements, Joe Stalin must have been turning in his grave. His shrewd diplomacy and well disciplined army had enabled him to impose Soviet-type communism on all the neighbouring countries and he plainly saw these as a screen to protect the Soviet Union against the West. Yet here were two young, active members of the Communist Party calmly telling us how these countries could be used as a convenient staging-place to out-manoeuvre the KGB and defeat the Soviet censorship.

Our friends, who had two small children, were proud possessors of a new flat. They had wangled their way to the front of the housing queue by bracketing themselves with her grandparents, who had been on the waiting list for many years. The parents of Lova and Natasha had their own homes so, although the new household spanned four generations of the family, it was inhabited by only three of them.

The flat had two bedrooms, one for Lova, Natasha and the baby, the other for the grandparents. There was a cupboard-size kitchen, a bathroom and a sitting-room which doubled as the little boy's bedroom. The balcony looked out over a wilderness which they hoped would soon be a garden.

The plumbing was primitive. In the lavatory there was a waste-paper basket placed by the seat. In the new buildings as with the old, lavatory paper, and particularly its coarser substitutes, cannot be flushed through the pipes. But although the supply of water was often cut off, Soviet standards of hygiene, judged by world rather than Western standards, rate fairly high. Tehran, capital of neighbouring Iran, which is far bigger than any Ukrainian city, has no sewage system at all.

Coming from Britain, we were staggered by the speed of the housing programme. Forty-five new homes were going up in Kharkov every day and we were told of one area which had been farm land in 1972 and was now a suburb housing 360,000 people. Inevitably, quality had been sacrificed to quantity. The new flats are composed of prefabricated rooms, with holes for the pipes and electric fittings. These ready-made rooms are delivered in huge containers and placed on top of each other by giant cranes. The homes are then supposedly ready for use. But, as Lova and Natasha soon discovered, the residents still have three choices: if they are competent in plastering, plumbing, electricity etc., they could do the finishing touches themselves; or they could live without modern conveniences; or they could pay – in money, kind or services – for skilled workmen to finish the job. The services of the odd-job man are very costly: he either does the job in his free time or, more frequently, takes time off his regular work, which means risking trouble.

Unfortunately for the Soviet Union, the increase in housing has not been matched by architectural innovations. Later we met a fully trained architect who had given up his profession and resigned himself to becoming a production engineer. He said that the general use of prefabricated housing units had almost eliminated the need for architects. The various ministries in Moscow which sponsor construction select a few models to satisfy nation-wide needs. The selection is often thrown open to competition from the architectural institutes all over the country. But once chosen, and with slight adjustments for varied climatic or geological conditions, the same buildings, in tens of thousands, go up all over the Soviet Union. That is why the cities are so alike.

As an example, the would-be architect described the plight of an unfinished holiday resort which we saw in the Crimea. It was being built for one of the prosperous collective farms, and several years previously the managers had been to Moscow and chosen the model. They had bargained about payment and knew there were unwritten laws about leaving a few rooms for Party members and for representatives from the ministry and the defence establishment. The building commanded a magnificent view over vineyards and sea, but construction had come to a standstill for lack of materials, labour and managerial drive. No one knew when the collective would have its 'sanatorium' – the Russian word for a collective holiday resort, though most of them are more like Butlins holiday camps than convalescent homes.

Cannot the collective, once it has paid, demand delivery? Apparently not. The allocation of labour and material is a matter of priorities, decided by the Party and the planners in Moscow. Extra money might help, but wrongly distributed, it could be dangerous.

The ugliness and uniformity of the new buildings was a most dismal aspect of our journey. Those who care for style and variety would have been better off in pre-Revolutionary Russia, when almost everyone with higher education and artistic discrimination, even if they had no money, could indulge in fantasy and eccentricity. But until the Revolution the educated were only a small minority. The Russian 1914 *Baedeker* reminds its well-to-do readers that 'Lower classes live in unspeakable poverty and destitution'. These 'lower classes' now have at least the hope of getting a modern flat and – if they are lucky – even a share in a holiday home.

7
Zaporozhye : Red Flags and Red Rivers

The 'unspeakable poverty and destitution' of the Russian working classes referred to by the *Baedeker* was conspicuously absent at our next stopping-place in Zaporozhye (pre-revolutionary Alexandrovsk). Since the Communists took over, it has grown from hardly more than a hamlet into a busy and highly industrialised metropolis. An Intourist pamphlet makes the point: 'Present-day Zaporozhye has nothing in common with the pre-revolutionary Alexandrovsk which O. Afanasyev-Chuzhbinsky, a writer and ethnographer of the last century, described as "a parody of a town". The best building it had then was the town jail packed full with prisoners.'

We did not see the prison. But under the Soviet system, unlike in the West, prisoners earn their keep. Common criminals are employed locally to supplement regular labour where it is in short supply in factories, mines, cement-works, and building sites. Political prisoners and recidivists are sent to the Gulag. Very few convicts would be sitting around in Zaporozhye.

Nor would anyone these days describe this throbbing metropolis as 'a wretched parody of a town'. But in the air they breathe and the water they use, the inhabitants pay a high price for progress. Zaporozhye has become a cautionary tale for ecologists.

Distance indicators are rare on Soviet highways and the first sign that we were approaching this conglomeration of over two million people was a thick yellow-grey cloud of smog hanging in a clear blue sky. The poison is in the water as well as in the air. Old people lament the days when the Dnieper and the Volga were famous for their fish. Now fresh water fish have virtually disappeared from the Soviet diet.

Until recently, Zaporozhye qualified as the U.S.S.R.'s most polluted city. 'You should have seen it five years ago!' said an internationally known physicist, who has published over thirty academic papers on pollution control in the Soviet Union. He has also published a book on his latest discoveries about methods of cleansing the atmosphere. The low priority attributed by the central powers to this branch of science is illustrated by the fact that the work was finished in 1974 but not published until 1977.

The city of Zaporozhye allocates 12 million roubles a year for its anti-pollution department, which is affiliated to the All Union Institute at Moscow. In these techniques the Soviet experts lead the world and Soviet patents have been sold on the international market.

The trouble, said the physicist, comes in the practical application of this knowledge in the steel-mills and the factories.

'But surely the Russians excel in applied physics? Look at the speed with which their scientific inventions have been transformed into weapons and space.'

'That's just the point,' he said. 'Defence gets absolute priority.'

In the Soviet defence establishment money, resources and manpower are no problem. Scientists work under tremendous pressure and one of them, Korolyov, the head of the rocket and space programme, is believed by his colleagues literally to have worked himself to death. Few can resist the immense rewards and prestige that go with military research and development. Jewish scientists are the only ones who sometimes refuse this kind of work as it permanently precludes emigration.

From the viewpoint of the majority of managers of Soviet plants and factories, cleansing the atmosphere is a luxury rather than a necessity. Central and local government have issued instructions and published decrees, fining offenders up to two million roubles for breaking the rules. But plant managers prefer to pay the fines from the budget of the enterprise rather than introduce expensive new systems which cannot be installed without interrupting production. For them the essential is the fulfilment, or better still 'overfulfilment', of the annual plan. The industrial bosses are all members of the Communist Party. They know that a failure to carry out the plan might cost them their jobs and even their Party membership – on which all their benefits and privileges depend. 'Overfulfilment' on the other hand is richly rewarded.

The smog could be quickly dissipated if the Politburo decided to enforce obedience to the anti-pollution rules. My physicist informant said that Russians and Americans had discussed selecting one city in each country and seeing how it could be cleansed. Zaporozhye may become a model town but meanwhile it still looks, and smells, dirty.

An angry young man, Stasha, active in the Zaporozhye Komsomol and a full member of the Communist Party, took us to see – and allowed us to photograph – a stream so polluted by an adjacent chemical factory that the water looked like blood. (The reader must take my word for it: all our photos were confiscated at the frontier on our way back.) The Intourist leaflet on Zaporozhye invites visitors to 'the bright blue waters of the Dnieper River'. But locally, the Dnieper is referred to as 'the red river'.

Industrial pollution is also a problem in the West. Left-wingers blame capitalist factory-owners, greedy for profits. Most Western parliaments have passed laws compelling manufacturers to take preventive measures and inspectors are sent round to see that the rules are obeyed. Such a solution would appeal to the Soviet author Vladimir Soloukhin, who has a lot to say about pollution in his fascinating book *A Walk in Rural Russia*, published first in Moscow and later translated and published in London. He travelled by foot and hitch-hiked in regions less than a couple of hours' drive from the capital and was remarkably frank about what he saw.

In the little town of Yuriev, east of Moscow, Soloukhin eavesdropped on a conversation between his girl-barber and a fellow client and heard that all the river fish had died after the introduction of a new dye in the local textile works. He went to the manager and asked how the effluent was purified. The manager said that a biofilter would cost 2 million roubles (which, Soloukhin observed, 'is no more than the cost of the front steps of a new building'). Instead, the factory used a method of raising the transparency of the water to satisfy the controllers. The process turned the liquid which poured out of the factory from ink-black to tea-brown. The water was still poisonous to man and beast.

Soloukhin observes, 'We sleep, we bury ourselves in our affairs and in the meantime, both day and night, hundreds of thousands of poisonous streams pour ceaselessly into our bright rivers and destroy all forms of life. Is it possible that this criminal disgrace should continue?

'Perhaps it is not the factories which should be fined, because this simply means that the state is fining itself; the fine should be on the managers. If they are made to feel it in their own pocket, they will take the matter in hand and our rivers will be purer.'

Soloukhin seems to be right; the rivers are purer in the West, where the capitalists would indeed feel the pain in their pocket.

But it is more than ten years since Soloukhin proposed his remedy and the Zaporozhye firms still prefer to pay fines rather than apply the anti-pollution devices. The Communist Party plainly prefers to pollute the atmosphere than to retard the plan.

According to Stasha, only one of the big industrial complexes has invested sufficient money and effort to solve the problem. This is a factory in the centre of the city, originally built to produce agricultural machines and owned by Germans. The Soviet authorities confiscated it and it now manufactures passenger cars. Stasha said it was the only local enterprise which recycled its water rather than dumping the waste straight into the river.

Physically polluted, Zaporozhye – at least in outward appearances – is ideologically pure. Everywhere there are promises and affirmations of the triumph of Communism. No other city we visited so vaunted its loyalty. Banners stretch across the highway; steel emblems are nailed to the lamp-posts; murals cover the sides of the multi-storey apartment buildings; slogans are spread over the tops of high buildings in giant letters. Night-time brings no relief: the symbols of party power and glory are lit up in multicoloured fairy lights, worthy of Blackpool.

The local Communist Party has certainly learned its lesson since 1946, when Leonid Brezhnev gave it a dressing-down for failing to make proper use of 'visual aids' to deliver its message to the people. The reprimand was delivered when Brezhnev came down to organise the city's reconstruction. He found Zaporozhye in ruins, without water, heating or light.

In the section entitled 'Rebirth' of his probably ghost-written autobiography, which is being published in separate instalments, Brezhnev says that he reorganised the Party and shifted the emphasis from economics to politics. The local cadres blamed the reconstruction delays on the lack of cement. 'I told them, don't concentrate on technical matters, concentrate on people.' (One could imagine Brezhnev might now be saying: 'Don't worry about biofilters, hang up more flags!')

Brezhnev's chapter was published in the literary monthly *Novy Mir* in May 1978 and became compulsory reading for Communist Party members (at least for those who could find it. When we were there it was sold out everywhere: I bought my copy back in London). Seminars were held all over the Ukraine so that Party members from different walks of life could meet, discuss their leader's experience and confirm that his advice had been taken to heart. Today no one, however short-sighted, indolent or illiterate, can complain of being deprived of visual aids.

Brezhnev cited the example of the Red Army during the 'Great Patriotic War', meaning the 1941–5 Russo-German War. Other battles in other parts of the world are rarely mentioned. While the Germans were still occupying the big Ukrainian cities, the Soviet troops in the forests carved morale-boosting slogans on the barks of trees: 'Kiev, next in the bag!' Now Brezhnev found the civilians falling down on the job: 'At the power dam, nothing! No slogans, no appeals, no names of leading workers. Not a single figure to show what we had accomplished nor what we were aiming for. ...'

Today the military tradition has been duly revived. The exhortations and panegyrics are in military style, with an emphasis on honour, strength, victory and glory. Even the brightly coloured posters urging international friendship show a clenched fist, a hammer and a Soviet flag.

In the Zaporozhye temple, Lenin is God and Brezhnev His prophet. Lenin never went to Zaporozhye but he is regarded as its creator. At a candlelit meeting of the Central Committee in Moscow, soon after the Revolution, standing in front of a great map of the country, he is said to have pointed to Alexandrovsk: *there* would be the location of the great hydroelectric dam essential for the building of Communism. On the hill above the dam stands what is probably the largest Lenin statue in the country. When we were there it was protected by an even larger steel net, to preserve Lenin against the stones and rocks hurled into the air by the engineering operations to widen the river and make it accessible to ocean-going ships.

Most of the conspicuous slogans are incantations to Lenin, such as 'Lenin, the honour and glory of our epoch!' or 'Lenin is knowledge!'. Zaporozhye is merely an extreme case of a nation-wide cult. After school, graduation, or a wedding, girls in virginal white come and lay carnations at the idol's feet. In comparison with Lenin, Brezhnev has a low – but currently rising – profile.

A recent manifestation of the cult of his personality was announced on Kiev radio shortly after we left. It said that a plaque had been unveiled in a Ukrainian village which reads: 'Here on the night of 11–12 December 1944 Leonid Brezhnev, head of the Political Department of the 18th Army, fired a machine-gun while beating off an enemy agent.' Brezhnev is the only other widely exhibited national leader, probably the only political face the Soviet man in the street would recognise.

Brezhnev was born and brought up at Dnieprodzerzhinsk, but his family name is Russian and in the list of deputies of the Supreme Soviet he is registered as of Russian nationality. The ethnic group of each Soviet citizen is registered on his identity card: if he comes of mixed parentage he can, when he comes of age, decide to which of the two groups he wishes to belong.

We had seen no pictures of Brezhnev in Lvov or in Kiev – which does not mean there were none. But in Zaporozhye his face, with an avuncular smile, beamed down from a hoarding five storeys high next to our Intourist hotel.

Our Intourist guide, Olga, gave an effusive account of what the Party, from Lenin to Brezhnev, had done for Zaporozhye. Olga would have qualified as an excellent public relations officer for any Western firm. Like all good sales staff she succeeded because she passionately believed in her product. She was a tall, handsome girl, well dressed and well shod, and she wore exquisite filigree gold ear-rings. Her bronze suntan, she said, was acquired during a recent cruise through the Black Sea and the Mediterranean as far as Malta. Though she spoke very good English, that was as far West as she had ever travelled.

Olga took us down the fifteen-kilometre highway, the Lenin Prospect – 'the longest road in the Ukraine, perhaps in the world'. She showed us the famous dam and said that industry was expanding so fast that more power was urgently needed. She pointed out the factory which produces 150,000 minicars a year and said that at 3,700 roubles (for the average worker, over two years' pay) they were 'the cheapest in our country'. All prices are fixed from Moscow but passenger cars are so scarce that it is supply rather than price that restrains demand. We heard of a man who paid 2,000 roubles just to get himself to the top of the waiting list, but had no legal recourse when the retailer moved with the cash to another town.

Olga showed us many ornate educational and cultural centres, including the new Palace of Sports. She took pride in telling us that the man who then held the world record in high jumping 'lives in our city'. We crossed a bridge to a green island exclusively reserved for recreation. She was anxious to show us a rehabilitation centre which she believed unique. It admitted workers who had physical or mental ailments but were fit enough to stay at their job. The patients were free of household chores and families and friends were kept away.

It was a hot sunny day and Margaret said she was parched. It was the first time in my life that I saw anyone refuse a request for a drink of water. A sturdy, matronly figure in white overalls came to the door, heard what we wanted and told us to get out. Olga was flustered and took us to a nearby canteen where, after some argument, we were served with fruit juice, free of charge.

Later, on one of our longer drives, Olga asked when the British elections were expected. Hoping to stimulate political argument, I said that some British feel that their first-past-the-post simple-majority system of voting discriminates against the minorities.

'In our country', said Olga, 'we have solved the minority problem.' She was referring to the representation of the ethnic minorities in the Supreme Soviet of Nationalities. She had no experience of a plural society and could not grasp the concept that minority *opinions* could have any right to representation.

The Soviet of Nationalities is one of the two Houses of Parliament set up under the Soviet constitution; neither does more than rubber-stamp decisions of the Politburo.

But even this stunted assembly does not truly represent the national groups within the USSR. Back in London I consulted a volume listing the deputies, together with their racial origin and their constituencies. Though it was dated 1966 there is no reason to think the present assembly is more ethnically representative. An Armenian, Rzaev, represented the mainly Muslim Azerbaijan. The well-known Russian-Jewish writer, the late Ilya Ehrenburg, represented Turkic Bashkir. And there were no less than five Abdullahs (one male 'Abdullayev' and four female 'Abdullayevas') representing four separate territorial units: Uzbekistan, Turkistan, Tadzhikistan and Azerbaijan. Ethnically, the five Abdullahs should have been grouped together, but the Russians resist any cohesion among the minorities groups by splitting them into small communities and encouraging linguistic and cultural peculiarities.

Olga was wrong: the Soviet Union has not solved the problem of minorities, either in the ethnic or in the social sense. In some cases, as in the West, deviants from the norm engage in criminal activities.

We were reminded of the fact when we took an afternoon off and switched on the television, which was showing a 'cops and robbers' play entitled 'The Militiamen'. The cops were brave, handsome, honourable; the robbers were grimy, greedy and vicious.

The hero is an innocent young man who has come to the city (unidentified) to enrol in the university. One of the local policemen, good and pure, is a boyhood friend. On his arrival at the railway station, the hero falls in with a gang who pretend to be fellow students and offer him help and hospitality. The gang leader boasts that he knows the university rector and can 'fix' the newcomer's admission. But the hero retorts: 'I prefer to enter the honourable way' (evidently viewers know there are dishonourable forms of access such as bribes and influence).

The gang invite him to a party, ply him with vodka, take him into the forest, beat him up (here the TV shows some very gory and sadistic details) and leave him half dead, gagged and bound – no papers, no money, and no prospects. A kindly chief of police tells him sadly that he will have to be sent back to his family. Luckily, at that moment, the young policeman enters and guarantees his friend's honesty, and the film ends with the two resolving they will work together to track the criminals down.

Though the 'goodies' and 'baddies' are as clearly identified as in a traditional Western, the viewers are invited to feel a twinge of sympathy for one member of the gang, who symbolises the fallen angel. He is a young student who has lost confidence in himself, taken to drink and, in spite of the supplications of his mother and sweetheart, falls into evil company.

But, for young people who want to let off energy in a non-collectivist way, Zaporozhye provides at least one outlet other than crime. They can go to 'The Cocktail Bar', a modified form of Western discothèque not far from the Intourist hotel. Foreign students staying in the hotel introduced us to some young Russians, and they invited us to join them for an evening at the club. The entrance fee was a rouble, which excluded the down-and-outs. Most of the boys and girls seemed to belong to the professional classes and were dressed in Western fashion. Instead of vodka and beer, which are the most common drinks, they could choose from a variety of cocktails which included 'cognac with liqueur', 'cognac with champagne', 'fizz cognac', and 'punch'. There were also mineral waters and fruit juices. The dancing was uninhibited, but there was no rowdiness or frenzy. The lighting was dim, the painting and sculptures abstract, the service personal and friendly. Tape music was mainly Western, with tunes from well-known pop groups, including Boney M and Abba.

More astonishing than the existence of this kind of discothèque in the heart of Zaporozhye was the fact that it had been initiated, sponsored and paid for by the local Komsomol – in other words by the youth movement of the Communist Party. The bar paid its way but the money for the premises and decorations came from the earnings of Komsomol members during their 'voluntary' Saturdays. ('Voluntary' in the Soviet vernacular does not mean that workers volunteer their services: only that they do not get paid for what they do.) The proceeds of Komsomol voluntary work supplements the regular labour force at building-sites, farms and factories. It is normally allocated to Communist activities and propaganda. Yet on this occasion the money was spent to allow Zaporozhye youth to enjoy Western-style pleasures, anathema to Party purists.

'Why ever', I asked, 'does the Komsomol encourage this kind of thing?' The answer was straightforward: 'We managed to persuade them it would be better to give our young people somewhere to spend their evenings rather than have them running loose in the streets.' After the television programme I saw the point.

We talked of the similarity of tastes and fashions of East and West and of the absurdity of conflict and collision. 'I sometimes dream of a world', said one of the young men, 'where people will just travel anywhere they like; Britain, France, the Soviet Union, Germany, and then freely make up their minds where they want to live.' In this location, the proposition sounded madly Utopian. But it brought home to me that even Zaporozhye – contrary to appearances – is not going the 1984 way.

I had booked an extra night at Zaporozhye, hoping that we could leave ahead of time to visit the famous nature reserve, Askania Nova. This was a 4½-hour drive to the south and only slightly off our route to the next scheduled stop, at Yalta. Askania was marked on the Intourist map, which implied that it was not banned for tourists – although the absence of a little bed next to a place-name meant there were no sleeping facilities. But the seats in our Volkswagen could be put into a reclining position and it would have been so easy to spend the night in the car: easy, but forbidden. Instead, we went all the way there, stayed three hours and came all the way back.

8

Askania Nova: Paradise Relost

Something funny was obviously going on in Askania Nova. The name was on the map of touristically accessible places and, as it was to be the topic of Margaret's thesis, we had particularly asked the London Intourist office to include it in the itinerary. 'Impossible, it is closed to foreigners while being reorganised.'

Organising Askania cannot be easy. This 10,000-hectare estate, north of the Black Sea and about half-way between Odessa and Rostov, has four functions difficult to combine.

The first, which makes it internationally famous, is the preservation in their pristine form of the flora and fauna.

The Soviet natural scientist, A. G. Bannikov, writes:

The steppe is magnificent. It is wonderful both in early spring, when it is strewn with red and yellow tulips, dark violet and yellow irises, and in summer, when it is wrapped up in the silvery-dove-grey smoke of feather-grass iridescent at the slightest breath of wind.

When the European feather-grass blooms, one can see among its tassels slender, graceful bunches of succulent-lilac steppe mullein; the small white flowers of sandwort, delicate pink carnations, and yellow salsify are hardly discernible. Here and there grow steppe umbellifers, and near the burrows of susliks grow flower-beds of greyish dove-coloured wormwood.

Later, in mid-June, after the feather-grass has blossomed, appear the fragrant caps of the yellow bedstraw, pyramidal white-tormentose sage, delicate lilac flowers on the spherical, spreading shrubs of sea-lavender, and onion-plants, and yellow steppe Centaurea begin to blossom. If the summer is humid, then the blossoming of European feather-grass in mid-June is replaced by the delicate, gold-coloured waves of long awns of *Stipa capillata* covering the steppe to its very horizon.

The steppe country in the Soviet Union once extended over hundreds of thousands of square miles. But, with the advance of the colonisers, intensive cultivation has damaged the texture of the soil and the herds of sheep have stamped down the earth, creating bogs in the winter and dust storms in the summer. Without sternly enforced protective measures, the steppe will vanish. A Ukrainian-born Britisher pointed out to me that whereas it may take hundreds of years to produce the lawn of an Oxford college, it takes thousands to create the steppe's communities of plant and animal life. Once the ecological balance is disturbed, the steppe cannot be artificially recreated.

Askania's second function is botanical. Thanks to a large number of artesian wells, a lush, multi-coloured oasis has been created in the middle of a largely treeless southern Ukraine. About a hundred years ago, a rare assortment of plants and birds was assembled from all over the world. The gardens are in the romantic tradition: glades, thickets, shrubberies, ponds and lakes, all contrived to look natural. The Askania park is probably as near to the Garden of Eden as anything this side of the grave – if only you can hear the warbling of the hundreds of different species of birds over the patter of the official guides.

Thirdly, there is the zoo, which deliberately excludes predatory species but possesses one of the world's biggest varieties of antelope, bison, buffalo and deer. Askania was the first breeding-ground for the famous Przhevalski horse, a fierce, untameable species, originally found in Mongolia – the last to survive in a natural environment.

Having heard about the Przhevalski's reputation, I had imagined a creature sleek and graceful as an Arabian steed. On the contrary, it has many of the attributes of a donkey: a huge head, a grey stocky trunk and short legs. Its special attribute is its long and bristly mane, which stands upright like crew-cut hair on a man's head. The species has great commercial value and zoos all over the world pay thousands of pounds for a single mare. But no one could call them beautiful.

Askania's fourth function is strictly utilitarian: providing land and livestock for a large experimental farm which occupies about three-quarters of the available land and specialises in cross-breeding. According to the Intourist guide, eighty-three new hybrid forms of beast and birds have been bred at Askania. The purpose of the farm is to extract more and better food, wool, leather and transport from the mixed breeds. To the Soviet administration, this fourth, agricultural function is the most important of all and the whole of Askania is now under the authority of the Ukrainian Ministry of Animal Husbandry. One major innovation is the creation of what is believed to be the only antelope farm in the world. An enormous eland weighing one ton provides unusually rich milk, claimed to contain unique medicinal properties, and widely used in Soviet hospitals.

As I gradually became aware, a bitter struggle is in progress between farmer and scientist for the control of Askania. At present the farmers are winning but the scientists have powerful friends and are fighting back. This unresolved contest was no doubt the 'reorganisation' to which the London Intourist office had referred. With a lifetime's experience of overcoming bureaucratic restrictions, I had no doubt that we would get to Askania and I arranged to book an extra day at Zaporozhye, the nearest city open to foreign tourists, and to arrange to go there when we arrived. The two places were 250 kilometres apart and, given the state of the roads, some five hours' driving.

Initially the name Askania meant nothing to me; it was for Margaret's sake that we included it in the tour. But before leaving London I read *Bagazh*, the vividly evocative autobiography of the composer Nicolas Nabokov, cousin of the writer Vladimir and nephew of Friedrich von Falz-Fein, the creator of the Askania nature reserve, park and zoo. The book made me as eager as Margaret to include the reserve in our tour.

Falz-Fein was born in 1863 and belonged to the German colony which had been invited by the Tsarina Catherine II to come to cultivate the steppes. When Falz-Fein was still in his twenties, he started drawing on the huge fortune amassed by himself and his family in sheep farming to buy a vast collection of animals and plants from all over the world. A comparable venture was going on at the same time on the other side of Europe in Woburn. Falz Fein corresponded regularly with the Duke and Duchess of Bedford of that period, who were engaged in a similar enterprise. According to the classic history of zoological gardens, *l'Histoire des ménageries de l'Antiquité à nos jours* by Guslave Loisel, by 1912 the Russian Empire, England and the United States were the countries with the biggest nature reserves. And in 1889 Friedrich von Falz-Fein set aside 1,563 hectares of the steppe to remain for ever unmowed and unpastured, in order to preserve its natural character. By the turn of the century Askania had secured an international reputation.

Nabokov writes:

Since my early days, Askania Nova has been on the lips of everybody around me. Tales of ostriches walking in the winter snow; cross-breeds of European and American buffalo with the Westphalian cow and wild horses from Tibet cross-bred with African zebras; green canaries turning white in the winter; gazelles and wild turkeys attending one's outdoor breakfast: all these stories were told and retold by everyone who had been to Askania Nova. No wonder that, to my childish imagination, Askania was a lost paradise, a Noah's Ark and a promised land.

In a series of holidays, young Nabokov's expectations were richly fulfilled. He recalls how much he enjoyed the simple, unfussy life with his uncle, who was too preoccupied with the animals and the estate to have time for the boring rituals of an aristocratic household. He remembers eating strange exotic food: a roast of buffalo, a rack of kangaroo, a huge pink carp. He evokes the clean and neat aviaries with Japanese-style gardens and miniature shrubberies that made the exotic birds feel at home. He records the endless stream of visiting scientists; some came for a week and stayed for a lifetime. Nabokov learned a special way of rubbing pieces of paper together which made the nightingales sing. And he watched uncle Friedrich offering his cigarette to a passing gazelle. In 1914, a few weeks before the First World War, Tsar Nicolas II went to Askania, admired the estate, and named Falz-Fein a baron – a title inherited and currently used by another nephew, Edouard von Falz-Fein, who now lives in Lichtenstein.

Came the Revolution. Friedrich was arrested and imprisoned in Moscow. Single-minded as ever, he proceeded to deliver lectures about Askania Nova for the benefit of his fellow inmates. According to Nabokov, the Communist leader Anatoly Lunacharski used to come to the prison to hear him. Lunacharski was one of the many intellectuals among the original Bolsheviks and they took land preservation very seriously. Soon after the Revolution, Askania was declared a national park, a new institute was built and the management was entrusted to Ivanov, a scientist who had formerly worked for Falz-Fein. The Institute is called after Ivanov and Falz-Fein became a non-person: the Askania museum contains no picture of its founder and no acknowledgement that the whole place was his creation.

In 1956 the search for knowledge became less urgent than the search for food, clothes and transport. It was then that Askania, including the Institute, was placed under the control of the Ukrainian Ministry of Animal Husbandry. The scientists had pressed their case and got it aired in Moscow's most important intellectual weekly, the *Literaturnaya Gazeta*. The first occasion was on 12 October 1977, with a four-page article on Askania by Nora Argunova. It was mainly a lyrical description of Askania's natural assets but it sternly denounced the management for its failure.

According to Argunova, there were three categories of despoilers: the shepherds, who grazed their destructive herds on the precious steppe; the tourists, who left rubbish around, plucked the flowers and brought in transistors which frightened the birds; and the poachers, who came by car, motor bike or scooter. Nora Argunova did not say, and perhaps did not know, that the Falz-Feins used to employ no less than 100 Cossacks, riding around with whips, to keep out intruders. But she does reveal that the present-day Askania has to rely for security on one lorry and two horse-drawn carts.

For the last ten years, Argunova says, the leading local expert, Evgenia Vedenko, 'has been fighting indefatigably' to warn the country that the virgin steppe is in imminent danger of extinction. In 1955 it was agreed by the Central Committee of the Communist Party of the Ukraine that the steppe reserve should be surrounded by a high wire fence and protected by a strip, one kilometre wide, of unirrigated no-man's-land. Yet six years later, in 1971, Vedenko was writing to complain that the state had 'neither the means nor the independence to implement these resolutions'. 'In consequence, our world-famous Askania is merely a subordinate branch of the local institute of animal husbandry'.

A later issue of *Literaturnaya Gazeta* published four letters from eminent scientists – three of them members of the USSR Academy of Sciences and one an official in the Academy's secretariat. All gave Argunova and Vedenko their unqualified support.

The first Academician, V. Sokolov, attributes 'the extremely bad state' into which Askania has fallen to the fact that it is managed by the wrong people. The second, M. Gilyarov, deplores the neglect of the treasures of Askania which for the natural scientist, he says, are comparable to those of Leningrad's Hermitage. The third, K. Sitnik, protests that the estate has already been reduced to one quarter of its original 40,000 hectares, and that neighbouring farms are still encroaching on its land. While expressing proper gratitude to the Ukrainian Communist Party, which in 1965 stopped any further ploughing of the Askania steppe, he nevertheless asks: 'What sort of well-being could be claimed for a nature reserve criss-crossed with lines of communication and into which shepherds bring their flocks, sometimes under the cover of darkness, sometimes shamelessly in broad daylight?'

Sitnik protests that 'the most outrageous violations of the

rules are perpetrated by the very people whose duty it is to enforce them' – presumably referring to the fact that the offending shepherds are employees of the Askania estate.

Yet, despite this flourish of eminent pens, the scientists have not yet got their way. Their discontent was conveyed to the last of the Falz-Feins, 66-year-old Edouard (the last surviving Falz-Fein male: his only child is a girl).

Nicolas Nabokov, visiting Moscow in 1962, refused an invitation to go back to his beloved Askania: he felt it would be too painful. Baron Edouard, on the other hand, who specialised in botany at the Alpes-Maritimes University, spent twenty years trying to get back. His villa at Lichtenstein is named 'Askania Nova' and he was in constant correspondence with Michael Kurdyuk, Askania's chief botanist.

The chance came in October 1978. Falz-Fein had been appointed a member of the Lichtenstein Olympic Games committee and became friendly with Sergei Pavlov, the Soviet Minister of Sports. A telephone call from so exalted a personage secured his immediate admission.

For the Ukrainian Communists the Baron's visit must have been highly embarrassing. They have systematically reviled his family. All visitors to the nature reserve are told that the founder was only interested in self-aggrandisement. The Falz-Feins are accused of exploiting their workers and 'charging them for every drop of water'.

The record suggests otherwise. The 1914 *Baedeker* describes Askania as 'a model estate'. Gustave Loisel notes that the Askanian workers were given ostrich eggs. And the Falz-Feins take pride in the splendid portraits of four former employees who outlived their centenary.

The Baron was warmly received by Kurdyuk, who went to Kiev to meet him, but he received only a cursory 'how do you do' and 'goodbye' from the Director of the Institute employed by the Ukrainian Ministry of Animal Husbandry. The local people moved him to tears by their hospitality, they plied him with gifts, especially jam, and he was hugged by an old woman who said she had once been a parlourmaid at his uncle's home. It is a revealing sidelight on the workings of the Soviet administration that, before his departure, Falz-Fein was approached by the scientific staff at the Institute and asked whether he – of all people – could use his Moscow contacts to help them win back Askania for science.

Unlike the Baron, we had no Olympic connections. Our first effort to reach Askania was made at Kiev and proved significantly unsuccessful. We called at the Ukrainian Academy of Sciences and asked to see the official who handled relationships with the outside world. A courteous but rather melancholy man told us we should call the next day. When we came back he was more melancholy than ever: the scientists could do nothing for us. Askania was outside their jurisdiction.

At Zaporozhye it was now or never. The answer at the Intourist counter was a predictable 'Nyet'. In difficulty, I always remember the advice given to me by the defector Guy Burgess, when I was *The Observer*'s Moscow correspondent: 'When you are up against petty bureaucrats, thump the table – otherwise they will give you hell.' During our tour, I lost my temper about once a day, mainly to good purpose, but this was the grand slam. After declaring that we had come all the way to see Askania I strode off and Margaret stayed behind and dissolved into tears.

They relented at least enough to refer the matter to their superiors, a rare concession as it was Sunday – superiors do not like disturbed weekends. When we returned that evening they announced that they had good news for us: we could go. But it would cost 63·5 roubles – which meant changing another £50. The entrance charge to Askania – complete with (compulsory) guided tour – is only 30 kopecks. Yet Intourist assured me that our excursion was not making them a penny profit. It was simply that the area is closed to foreign cars and to unescorted foreigners. We had to pay for a private car, driver and guide. As we would be travelling for nine hours and hoped to spend at least three at Askania, the driver and guide would have to be paid for a twelve-hour day.

This was no time for horse-trading. I went to the cash desk, where a young lady was sitting with an electric calculator on her right and (presumably as a fall-back) an abacus on her left. She changed the money, I paid Intourist and retired early to bed, to be ready for a long, hard slog.

Next day, as we got into our Volga, the spacious Soviet-made limousine, Olga, who was again our guide, congratulated us upon our good fortune: it was more than two years since any foreigners had been admitted to Askania. A party of Australians had been turned back after driving all the way from Moscow. Why? The local Intourist office had not been told that reorganisation was the official excuse. Olga said that foreigners were quarantined in order to protect the livestock from infection. Thousands of visitors from all over the Soviet Union visit Askania every month yet we were asked to believe that only people without Soviet passports are health hazards.

The day began with a heavy downpour of rain and hail and the roads turned into slush. In less than an hour we saw four accidents – lorries that had fallen into a ditch, collided or overturned. The road surface was not the only problem. Most of the drivers were peasants, brave but relatively new to motor transport. It is still something of a game: they drive recklessly, never signal their turns and race each other as if their lives depend on getting there first.

In the West, danger spots are marked by red flags. In the Soviet Union, red flags carry another meaning and the Russians have chosen a more dramatic way of conveying the message. The police select mangled and demolished cars taken from real accidents, and then hoist them as a warning signal on big boulders by the side of the road. Do these sinister symbols help? Perhaps they do. Anyway, the little Volkswagen survived many storms without a crash.

As we neared Askania, the sun came out, the fields were covered in mauve foxglove and everything seemed radiantly inviting. Neither our driver nor Olga knew the route; we took a wrong turning and drew up outside the massive buildings of the experimental farm. It was annexed to the local petrol station and surrounded by a dirty farmyard with straggling poultry. We were quickly shooed away and after a few more kilometres we were in the real steppe: tall, silvery-grey grass separated from the road by a narrow strip of bare earth. We caught a glimpse of a herd of deer – and that was all of the nature reserve we ever saw.

The car stopped at a barrier. We got out and went to an

office conspicuously marked EXCURSBURO, in Russian and Roman characters. The Russians favour abbreviations: 'agitprop' (agitation and propaganda), 'Politburo', 'Ovir' (the office where would-be emigrants plead for their exit visas). The sinister-sounding EXCURSBURO was the office for guided tours.

Olga said we were not part of any group and she went into the Ivanov Institute to arrange an escort. The Institute, built in 1923, is decorated with Communist Party slogans and has a front colonnade of massive pillars.

The pillars, I discovered later, had been taken from the church which the Falz-Feins built for the local congregation. They – and the rest of the German colony – were Lutheran; the peasants were Orthodox. The church was ecumenical: the two faiths took turns at the altar.

Opposite were prefabricated buildings which included a non-*de-luxe* hotel (hot water once a week). If we had been allowed to stay there we could have saved nine hours of driving.

Olga came out with a woman named Zoya Konstantinovna Polishchuk, who was a laboratory technician and took us on what was obviously the regulation tour, beginning with the huge war memorial to Soviet partisans. Fortunately it is concealed by trees from the rest of the 200-acre park. We started with a potted history denigrating the Falz-Feins. We were told, among other things, that they kept these treasures to themselves whereas the Communists threw them open to the general public. Should I have corrected her? The *Baedeker* for 1914 said that any travellers could go to Askania, provided they gave advance notice. In other words, permission was easier then than now. Further, as Uncle Friedrich had told Tsar Nicolas II, he employed ten full-time guides to take round visiting scientists and groups of tourists, particularly schoolchildren.

Mrs Polishchuk got her story from the printed guide published in 1965 in five languages – Ukrainian, Russian, English, French and German – which we were given before leaving. It asserts: 'Unfortunately the owners of the reserve were not guided by scientific aims in developing their farm. Being petty (as petty as the Duke of Bedford?) capitalist proprietors, they strived (*sic*) for the only interest: to surprise their guests with a rich and exotic collection of plants and animals.' I kept quiet.

From the gardens we went into the zoo, which for me was a mild disappointment and for Margaret, who is sentimental about animals, an outrage and violation of animal rights. We had expected a vast and exotic Whipsnade where we would see animals roaming over the steppe.

The animals on view were enclosed between small concrete partitions with a few rocks piled up in the sectors reserved for goats. The sad spectacle was the zebroids, half horse, half zebra, on which Askania scientists have been experimenting ever since 1908, but which are still incapable of producing offspring. These impotent creatures stood around looking miserable: no use to anybody, not even to each other.

After the guided tour we still had another hour and a half. Could we see the animals on the steppe? 'I cannot show you what it not allowed to be shown,' said Mrs Polishchuk with implacable logic. We went into the Ivanov Institute where there were charts on the wall showing, in upward curves, that the Askania beasts were producing more, better and faster than ever before.

The other tourists were mainly children in uniform from the pioneer camps. Most were marching in crocodile, behaving far better than their contemporaries in any Western zoo. One group of little boys were pressing their noses against the window of a closed refreshment bar, scanning the bottles to see if there was any Pepsi-cola. Alas, though Pepsi is now bottled not very far away from Askania it is not on the delivery route.

We joined the children in a small cinema near the entrance to see a film about Askania birds. It snapped in the middle and we walked out before they repaired it. As we came out into the afternoon sunshine the spectacle was tantalising: there was so little they would allow us to see.

But I am pleased we visited Askania. At least we had enjoyed the gardens, seen a little patch of virgin steppe and acquired some idea of the difficulties besetting the Soviet scientists. On problems of conservation, the Russian natural scientists can count on sympathy from their equally frustrated Western colleagues – not least from the British, who are failing to protect their own moors and dunes. The moral of the trip was: ecologists of the world, unite.

By mid-afternoon we were back on the Zaporozhye road knowing we would be retracing the route for another four hours the following morning and, for the fourth time, on our way back to Kharkov. But there was nothing we could do about it. We were required to spend another night at Zaporozhye before setting out for the Crimea. And the Crimea was especially important to me as I had promised my sister, Renée Soskin, mother of six and widow of a Russian Jew, that I would discover if there was anything left of the little village of Taganash, where he was born and spent the first years of his life.

9
The Ghost of Taganash

We never found Taganash, though according to the 1914 *Baedeker*, we must have passed very near it. It is mentioned as the first railway stop after crossing the isthmus into the Crimean peninsula. All *Baedeker* says is that it had a restaurant. We never found that either. Having accustomed ourselves to the fact that there would be no inns along the road, and driven for so long through land-locked territories, we had planned a picnic by the sea. We brought along our usual simple fare: locally produced bread, butter and cream cheese; sardines and concentrated black-currant juice bought in Austria; and a rouble's worth of cherries purchased from peasants along the road. As soon as we saw the sea we leapt out of the car – and then promptly leapt back in again. The isthmus passes between the Azov Sea and a putrid lake and it smelt as though a stink bomb had just gone off.

Until you climb the steep hills in the Southern part of the peninsula there are no signs of the vaunted attractions of the Crimean Riviera. The landscape in the north of the peninsula is dull and flat, the road bound in by hedges and trees, and this stage of our journey was memorable only because, for the first time, we had the companionship of a Soviet hitch-hiker.

In the Soviet Union people do not stand along the road, as they do in the West, waving placards to indicate their destination. Driving in other people's cars is arranged and paid for. In the towns, if there are no taxis or buses, you hail a private driver and if he is going your way you pay according to the local taxi fare. For longer journeys you can go by lorry and arrange to sit beside the driver. Officially, the payment is supposed to be in vouchers, not in money.

The woman we picked up at the northern tip of the Crimea was standing by a police station, where all traffic was halted and documents examined. While the militiaman was looking at ours, she was fussing about missing an important seminar at Simferopol, which was on our route. I invited her to come with us and she asked the militiaman's permission. First he said no, she should not trouble foreign visitors. She insisted it was Party business, we said we should be delighted to have her, and he relented. We cleared some of the baggage off the back seat and in she climbed. She told us that the Simferopol gathering was one of the meetings throughout the country to enable representatives from various professions to meet and discuss the Brezhnev memoirs. She *had* to be there on time.

It was a burning day and we stopped for rest and refreshment at a clean-looking café near a petrol station. As in all Soviet public eating-places, the manager did not risk setting out the cutlery, for fear of theft. But each table was laid with mats and glasses and a little vase of flowers. At first, our passenger stood waiting stoically outside in the sun. Then Margaret prevailed on her to join us, but she sat nervously at the edge of her chair, refusing all offers of food and drink.

Everything she said to us was so orthodox that it could have been blared out at the KGB headquarters. But she was uneasy and it took a long time before she unwound. When she did she told us all about herself: she worked as a journalist on the newspaper at Dzhankoy, a small town near where we picked her up. She pointed to the dreary-looking block of flats where she lived with her mother and one small son. If her husband had not deserted her, she would have liked many children. I told her about my sister's husband and asked if there were any Jews left in the Crimea. 'You have one sitting behind you,' she replied. Her mother had escaped before the Germans arrived and she had been born in Tashkent. They were happy to be back again and found the Crimea much preferable to Central Asia.

'Are there any Tartars left in the Crimea?' I asked.

'Yes, we have a Tartar woman writing on our paper. She composes beautiful poems about Soviet partisans.'

The reply astonished me. Tartars and Tartar-speaking Jews were in the Crimea long before it was annexed by the Russians in 1783, and I asked if she had ever heard of the Tartar-named village of Taganash. She said it had probably been absorbed into one of the big collectives. Later during our stay in the Crimea I made other and equally unavailing inquiries. One kindly man took down my address and said he would consult the records: I never heard from him.

Later I learnt that it was not only Taganash but all Tartar place-names that had been erased from the map. The decision to eliminate the names followed the deportation in May 1944 of all Tartars – men, women and children – previously constituting about one quarter of the Crimean population. They were sent to Central Asia as soon as the Red Army reconquered the territory from the Germans and the conditions of the journey were so terrible that almost half are reported to have perished along the way.

The Tartars were highly skilled market gardeners. The fertility of the Crimea has never recovered from their departure. My sister's father-in-law from Taganash spent the later years of his long life in England. It was a family joke that if you offered the old man fruit or flowers he would always say how much bigger and better they were in the Crimea. We saw no prize products in the Taganash region. The collective farms were strung along the road which was cluttered up with army lorries bringing in soldiers to help with the harvest.

Of all the ethnic groups accused by Stalin of collaborating with the Fascists, the Tartars were the last to be rehabilitated: in other words the deportation of the Tartars, as of other peoples, had been an error. The Volga and Crimean Germans were cleared in August 1964 but the decree withdrawing the collective charge against the Tartars was not published until September 1967. This does not mean that they may now come home. They need permits to leave their place of work, and permits to return to their previous homes. These are hardly ever granted. The official excuse is that their place has been taken by other ethnic groups, though until recently the authorities were still trying to recruit Ukrainians to inhabit empty land. Indeed, the use of soldiers to help with the harvest suggests there is still a shortage of labour. The likelier reason is the fear of a cohesive Muslim community in such a strategically vital area. There is perhaps also a sense of historical revenge. For centuries, the rulers of Muscovy had to pay tribute and prostrate themselves before the mighty Tartar princes.

If it was true that the Tartar poetess, of whom our passenger spoke, dedicated her talents to writing about Soviet partisans, she must have had a singularly forgiving nature. But, as I listened to our passenger, I became increasingly convinced that the poetess was just part of an entirely imaginary society in which we were asked to believe, where the multi-ethnic peoples of the Crimea all lived happily together. She pushed the image beyond the level of credibility. We know that life on the collective farms is less appalling than it was in Stalin's time. But she would have had us believe that today the peasants are spoilt: 'They all own good houses and have their own cars. ...' We were driving along the Moscow–Yalta highway and by Soviet standards there was an unusually large number of passenger cars. But they certainly did not belong to the local farm hands.

Why did our passenger make such extravagant claims? Was she just a dedicated Communist, lying for the glory of the Party? Or did her Jewishness make her feel that she must constantly be reaffirming her loyalty?

We hear a lot in the West about the Jews in the Soviet Union who wish to emigrate. Few people can fail to be impressed by their courage and endurance. As soon as they ask to leave for Israel they lose their jobs, their incomes and their physical security: they are liable to be beaten up by KGB thugs and deprived of police protection to themselves, their families or their property. Worse still, their children may be insulted and bullied by schoolmates, officially encouraged to treat them as subhuman. Further, those who have offended the authorities by campaigning for human rights are sometimes subject to physical torture. A detailed account of particular cases has been revealed, extensively and incontrovertibly, by Professor Peter Reddaway in his study of political prisoners in Soviet psychiatric hospitals.

But this should not obscure the fact that most Jews in the Soviet Union will remain there for the rest of their lives and many have resigned themselves to making the best of a bad job. Like our hitch-hiker, some are managing to participate actively in Soviet institutions. The figures for the membership of the Communist Party of the Soviet Union are revealing. Of the approximately three million Jews in the Soviet Union, in 1976 there were 294,774 listed as Party members. They constituted almost 2 per cent of the whole Soviet Communist Party, whereas Jews number just over 1 per cent of the total Soviet population.

This does not mean that they, any more than gentile members of the party, necessarily – or indeed probably – believe in the Communist creed. It is only that in the Soviet Union today ambitious people, believing or otherwise, join the Party, just as all over Europe in the Middle Ages they joined the Church.

The Kremlin seems undecided whether to treat the Jews as enemy aliens or as assimilated Soviet citizens who owe their loyalty to Moscow. Swings in policy could either be a case of schizophrenia or else a split within the leadership on the practical issue of whether a pro-Jewish or anti-Jewish policy is in the best interests of the Soviet Union. Perhaps the rational and irrational phenomena exist together: the Russian leaders both hate and admire the Jews and they are also divided between themselves on how to treat them.

Soviet policy towards the Jewish minority is certainly inconsistent and unpredictable. As I saw in Kiev, there is no memorial to the Jews who died at Babi Yar. But in the autumn of 1978 the literary world was astounded when the magazine *Oktyabr*, traditionally representing the most illiberal and hardline faction of the Party, serialised a moving wartime chronicle of a loyal and patriotic Jewish family, set in the Ukraine, where anti-Semitism has been traditionally at its worst.

In the Soviet Union, the definition of Jew (*yevrey*, as our passenger called herself) is purely ethnic. As early as 1928 Stalin tried to cut the Soviet Jewry away from the international Jewish community by settling them in a territory of their own inside the Soviet Union. The 'Jewish Autonomous Region' (in reality a district governed from Moscow) was set up in

Birobidzhan, an outpost in the Far East in the province of Khabarovsk, not far from the Chinese frontier. Unknown to most of the international Jewish community, it still exists, under the same name, and now has a population of about 200,000. Very few of them are Jews. In 1966, the 'Jewish Autonomous Region' was represented in the USSR Soviet of Nationalities by one Jew, one Ukrainian and three Russians.

When Soviet writers wish to designate those who profess the Jewish religion they prefer the word *iudey*. These represent only a small, though reputedly growing, fraction of Soviet Jewry. In the entire country, only ninety synagogues are allowed to function, most of them in inconspicuous little buildings.

One of the greatest left-wing fallacies nailed by the Communist Revolution is that, by abolishing the private sector of the economy, racial and ethnic divisions are eliminated. No one more fervently believed and spread this foolishness than Leon Trotsky. In his book *Warrant for Genocide* Professor Norman Cohn recounts how a deputation of Jews called on Trotsky during the Civil War to ask him to refrain from actions which would provoke the White soldiers to pogroms (by that time about 100,000 Jews had been massacred). Trotsky replied: 'Go home to your Jews and tell them I'm not a Jew and don't care about the Jews or what happens to them.' He would have had to care now, as he would have had his Jewishness stamped on his identity card.

Racial discrimination, of which anti-Semitism is unquestionably a form, is forbidden both in the USSR constitution and in the United Nations' declaration of human rights, which the Soviet Union endorsed. Nonetheless, in the Soviet Union today, particularly in the academic world, being a Jew is a serious handicap. The reasons for this are partly social. There are new classes of Russians, Ukrainians, Byelorussians and other residents of the European parts of the Soviet Union who now have secondary education and aspire to enter those professions formerly dominated by Jews. This is particularly true of the scientific and medical communities. The pressure is now acute because in the last twenty years, while there has been a vast expansion in the number of secondary schools, there has been a virtual standstill on the construction of new institutions of higher learning. In the desperate scramble for the limited university places, the ethnic factor has become crucial.

Privately, the authorities will argue that the object is only to reduce the proportion of Jews in the professions to the proportion they represent in the Soviet population. But as the Jews have occupied such a large place in most of the professions, this means that in practice, for many years to come, hardly any of the younger generation of Jews will be able to get into universities. Today only those with influence, money, or overwhelming intellectual powers can overcome the ban.

Later at Ordzhonikidze in the Caucasus, we met a bright young Jew who was celebrating his medical graduation. His family came from Odessa (he told us they spoke Yiddish at home) and he could have received a far better medical training if he had been admitted into one of the Odessa institutions. But for a Jew, Ordzhonikidze* was better than nothing.

Discrimination of this kind is not an innovation introduced by the Communists. Had it not existed in Tsarist times, my parents would probably not have emigrated and I would have been born in Russia. The situation at the turn of the century is remembered by an 89-year-old Jew, born and brought up at Kerch in the Crimea, who now lives at Juan-les-Pins. He and his brothers went to an assimilated Russian gymnasium but when they wanted to proceed to university they had to leave the country. He decided to become a doctor and studied medicine in Berlin.

The old man still recalls a pogrom which he is convinced was incited by Tsarist ministers, in which Cossacks burst into

---

* This is the capital of the North Ossetian Autonomous Republic (as with other similarly named Soviet territorial entities, neither autonomous nor a Republic). Until 1939 it was named Vladikavkaz, meaning 'mistress of the Caucasus', as it commanded the entrance to the military highway to Tbilisi. Ordzhonikidze was one of the old Bolsheviks who disappeared during the purge. Officially he died of heart failure but in his 1956 report Khrushchev said that Ordzhonikidze had been forced to shoot himself. Stalin must have wanted to cover his tracks by awarding his victim the posthumous honour of having this important place named after him. Vladikavkaz had been founded as a military garrison but by 1914 was also a mountain resort which boasted five internationally recognised hotels and a mountaineering club.

Kerch, looting and killing, and in which two of his school-mates were slaughtered in the streets. His family were relatively wealthy but this would not have protected them had it not been for the fact that the first floor of their luxurious apartment block happened to be inhabited by a Russian admiral.

Unfortunately, streaks of the old savagery still survive. The head of the department of physics at one of the Kharkov institutes, who had been drinking too much, told a Jewish subordinate that his own father had been a Cossack who used to beat up the Jews and that he, his son, would know other ways of beating them up.

Present day anti-Semitism in the Soviet Union is certainly a left-over from Tsarist times. All that can be said of the present regime is that, instead of fighting against it, they have been inclined to turn it to their advantage. A Russian-speaking executive of ICI recalls talking to a man browsing in a Moscow bookshop. 'What do you do?' 'I am the responsible Jew.' 'What does that mean?' 'Didn't you know? The Jews are officially responsible for all the miseries of the Russian people.'

In the academic world, a good deal depends on the people in charge. The American journal *Science* has noted the damage inflicted on Jewish mathematicians by the anti-Semitism of one eminent Russian, Lev Semenovich Pontryagin. As head of the editorial board of the main Soviet mathematical journal between the years 1970 and 1977, he reduced contributions by Jews from one third of the total to zero.

Not long ago, at Kharkov, the Soviet scientific community was rocked by the *skandal* (Soviet word to describe a big row) at its anti-pollution institute. Its head was a well-known Russian physicist and specialist in metallurgy, Sergey Michaylovich Andonyev, who liked working with Jews. Jewish physicists flocked into the Institute, which was enormously successful and began selling patents internationally. It was an almost entirely Jewish preserve and, when emigration became possible in the 1970s, several members of the staff asked to leave. Not all those who applied were allowed to go, but the notional exodus was sufficient to discredit Andonyev and the Institute was closed to Jewish scientists.

In the international arena, the Russians are embarrassed by their record and try to explain it away by arguing that their hostility is against 'Zionism', not against the Jews. In practice the two attitudes easily merge. The link between the anti-Israel and the anti-Jewish attitudes is well illustrated in a cartoon published in the Kiev satirical journal *Perets*. It depicts 'World Zionism' subverting détente and financing Israeli 'aggression'. The Jews in the picture have the symbolic hooked nose and the caption reads: 'Like father, like son' (*see opposite*). A Black Book collating illustrations of Soviet anti-Semitism was recently published by the Institute of Jewish affairs in London. All the material must have had the approval of the Soviet censor.

The notion of a great international conspiracy, in which the Jews are plotting to take over the world, has its roots in pre-revolutionary Russia. The history of the 'demonology myth' has been documented by Professor Norman Cohn in *Warrant for Genocide*. He links it with the mass hysteria of the Middle Ages which led to the burning of alleged witches. It was brought into Germany after the Revolution by the White Russians and seized on by Hitler.

There are signs that the demonology myth is now being revived. One of its chief propagators is Vladimir Yemelianov, whom the Soviet authorities permit to make speeches affirming that the Zionists plan to seize the world by the year 2000. He suggests it may need another world war to stop them. Yemelianov is the Soviet link-man with the PLO and the anti-Jewish campaign, in this case, can be linked with Soviet pro-Arab foreign policy. Moscow may also want to ingratiate itself with its own Muslim peoples: the USSR is now the fifth biggest Muslim state in the world.

Yet, strangely, despite the dreadful uncertainties looming over the Jewish population and the serious risk that once again they may be victims of what Hitler called 'the final solution', we met Soviet citizens who thought that the Jews were the lucky ones. Of all the Soviet ethnic minorities their right to emigrate has been most widely recognised. Soviet officials abroad argue that the international ballyhoo about the Jews is counterproductive and encourages the logical reluctance to offer them higher education in Soviet establishments: why

give them knowledge and skills they may later place at the disposal of an alien, perhaps enemy power?

But, inside the Soviet Union, people believe that external pressures do influence Soviet policy. In one town I met a non-Jew who was speaking somewhat incautiously about dissident writers. He said laughingly that if he got into trouble he would expect us to demonstrate in front of the Soviet Embassy in London. I promised I would.

The emigration option has encouraged a lot of Russian intellectuals to discover hitherto unmentioned Jewish relatives and antecedents. Further, there is now a high price on a Jewish girl willing to contract a formal marriage to help a gentile who wants to leave the country. One Georgian was offering a potential Jewish bride more than 5,000 roubles. The money cannot be taken out of the country but can at least protect the family which remains behind. In the Georgian's case, the girl refused, having been advised that the risk was too high. The Georgians, I was told, are wealthier than the Russians and a Jewish (non-functional) bride from Moscow or Leningrad can be had for only 3,500 roubles.

The woman in our car was certainly not a barterable bride. Her pro-Party patter gradually dried up and she was evidently increasingly worried that she would be late for her seminar. We offered to deliver her to the door of the meeting-place but she recoiled. Her arrival at a gathering of this kind in a Western car driven by representatives of the capitalist world would have been inappropriate. At her own request we left her at the first crossroads as we entered Simferopol.

10

The Black Market on the Black Sea

We drove straight through the prosperous looking city of
Simferopol and were soon climbing into the mountains up a
wide and shiny black road. The surface was so smooth and
well finished that we might have been going through some
new sea-side development area in the West, had it not been for
the wiring for trolley-buses, that went all the 75 kilometres to
Yalta. For the vast majority who have no cars, the trolley-bus
is the main vehicle.

When we saw the sea, the view was as lush and romantic as
anything on the French or Italian Rivieras – sudden steep
descents, broken by orange or cypress groves, vineyards, bare
rocks, thick woods, jagged promontories and mock castles
perched on crags, jutting into the sea.

Yalta is an enchanting little town, much of its prettiness
surviving from Tsarist days when it was already a fashionable
watering-place. As usual, our destination was kept from us as
a state secret, but there was a huge hotel dominating the
skyline, and we guessed that this was the place. We spent the
better part of an hour manoeuvring through tangled and
twisty lanes, which all seemed one-way in the wrong direction,
and at last made our way up the drive. The Hotel Yalta, as it
was called, is an eleven-storey building and its roof is topped
with a huge model of a sailing-boat. It can house and feed
3,500 people. It is Yalta's newest and biggest hotel and was
built by Yugoslav labour to a Yugoslav design.

It had been a tiring day and we staggered gratefully towards the reception desk. But our relief was short-lived. The Hotel Yalta did not cater for *de luxe* customers. It took another complicated excursion before we found the Oreanda hotel, by the shore, at the bottom of a dead-end road. This was a far older establishment, already listed in the 1914 *Baedeker*. It lacked the asterisk which the guidebook used to denote hotels which, in the editor's view, were 'well managed, reasonable and adapted to modern requirements'. The Oreanda still falls short of asterisk standards.

Once again we were given a spacious suite with a huge refrigerator. But our apartment did not quite qualify for top grade as it did not look out on the sea but on drab buildings. It was the Poles, we later discovered, who were the big spenders. They had the best rooms and occupied a large part of the private beach. This was not altogether surprising. In Warsaw I had heard that Polish families who spent their holidays on the Black Sea came back with more money in their pockets than when they left. The Poles have two commodities which the Russians want. First, they make higher-standard clothes, notably women's underwear, tights, brassieres and knickers. Second, those who have generous American relatives – of whom there are many – can receive dollars, keep a dollar bank account, and so buy Western-made goods available in the hard-currency stores. These can be resold at enormous profit.

If a Pole crosses the frontier into the Soviet Union he is less rigorously searched than a Westerner and there is no limit to the layers of undergarments his wife can wear. To encourage the officials to speed up the control processes, Polish parents urge their children, when they reach the frontier, to be as raucous and troublesome as possible.

But from the point of view of the big-time black marketeers who work the Black Sea beat, the holiday-making Poles are generally disappointing. On the way south Polish families stop at Kiev where the prices are higher; by the time they reach the coast, they have nothing left to sell and only roubles to pay for what is obtainable.

The disappointing performance of the Poles was described to us by Anton, who works not at Yalta but at Sochi, the other major Black Sea resort. But he said his colleagues in all the resorts had similar experiences. Anton is an Armenian and his principal trade was through the Yugoslavs who plied pleasure boats along the Black Sea coast. During their usual tours of duty, the captains were willing both to take orders and to deliver goods. Anton was a fat, middle-aged man, a sort of non-violent 'godfather'. He had a network of people working for him, including barmen, beach photographers, taxi drivers, and even gypsy children, less likely than adults to attract police attention. He was registered as a waiter.

Anton said that there is a lot of loose cash circulating in the sea-side resorts. Many Soviet citizens earn big money in Siberia and Central Asia and come to the Black Sea to blow it. He told us of innocent Uzbeks, who made a fortune by overproducing their quota of cotton, and who arrive loaded. Card-sharps are everywhere, and their victims often lose their last kopeck on their first night's stay. In Sochi, Anton led a remunerative but risky life. He had not dared to marry, found a family, or run his own car – though he always had willing drivers. He had bought a plot of land but had not yet built the residence he could afford. He was nervous, something of a hypochondriac, and did not think he could survive the three years' forced labour in the cement-works, which, he said, was the usual penalty for a first offence.

We made it clear from the start that we had nothing to sell and no intention of breaking the rules. But none the less he offered us hospitality and we asked him in return to accept the present of a few packets of Western cigarettes. He laughed at us. He said he had Western cigarettes coming out of his ears! We had better keep ours for times when we might need them.

In Yalta, the Oreanda Hotel has a disagreeable system of segregating foreign from Soviet clients. In the foreigners' dining room the service was better but the band, the dancing and the jollity were all on the other side of the wall. It was only the next morning that, while sunbathing, we made friends with Russian holidaymakers. We were invited out to a standard Russian lunch, bortsch soup and pork schnitzel, at one of the many eating-places along the front; and to dinner at the old sailing boat, the *Hispaniola*, converted into a restaurant. Luckily we had rejected an Intourist suggestion that we should dine there by ourselves: it would have been expensive and the Intourist clients were served in a stuffy enclosed cabin. Instead, our young friends arranged to have two barrels placed in the bow. Here we were served caviare, smoked sturgeon and the better quality of Georgian champagne, and we had about our only gourmet evening of the tour.

Most of the Soviet Union has a harsh climate and the trouble with the Black Sea beaches is that they are nowhere near extensive enough to satisfy the growing number of Soviet citizens – notably those working in Siberia – who want, and can now afford, the Riviera-type holiday. Even Coney Beach and Southend in their peak seasons cannot compare with the hugger-mugger density of crowds in the Russian holiday resorts. People pay astronomic prices for a bed in a dormitory accommodating as many people as space permits.

At the Oreanda we had our own private beach and each bather was entitled to a standard wooden plank with raised headrest on which to stretch. By noon all these were lined up in rows, touching one another. As for the public beaches nearby, they looked like the rush hour on the London tube: there was no space to sit, let alone to lie down. Yet people seemed not to mind; there were noisy sounds of merriment, guffaws of laughter, unexpected splashings, shrieks of joy. Never in touristic history have so many people enjoyed themselves so much – and as far as we could see so innocently – in such a confined space.

Some of the open beaches rent out their own wooden planks on a first come, first served basis. One group of girls travelling together took it in turns to get up at 4 a.m. to queue for the 9 a.m. opening. They did not complain: they were having a marvellous time and were beautifully bronzed. We went with some of them to the Luna Park fair, with merry-go-rounds, giant wheels and the usual assortment of pedlars, fortune tellers and other minor manifestations of private enterprise. We also went to the open market, which tended to be cleaned out as soon as it opened. I heard women shoppers complain that there were not even any cabbages left, and for the Russians cabbage is a standard food.

In the evening, we were invited to the Yugoslav emporium. What astonished us most was to see so many people in so many bars, so sober and so staid; it was as if they were still at school and not very far away from the master's study. The people who can really let themselves go, in the Russian style, are the lucky ones whose status or wealth gives them access to the old palaces and new villas which have private beaches, in and around the town. For the non-privileged, the best way of seeing Yalta's real attractions is to travel with field-glasses by boat. From the road, high walls or trees prevent the passers-by from peering in to see how the other half lives.

After our brief halt at Yalta we had three days of almost continuous driving. The restrictions on foreign tourists forced us to trace an enormous triangle: first we went north back to Zaporozhye and Kharkov; then south-east to Rostov. Both north and south, the routes were highways, linking the coast with Moscow. This meant that the road surfaces were better than earlier but the traffic was far worse.

In the final stage we went through the familiar detritus left by the first phase of the industrial revolution. The lower valley of the Don, where industry is a century old, is scarred with coal tips, dilapidated factories, decrepit-looking people and exhausted quarries. Reaching Rostov was a great relief: it provided the best hotel of our tour and the most interesting of the Intourist guides.

11

Rostov with Akhmet

'My name is Akhmet,' said our guide in the regulation Intourist style: no patronymic (with which Russians normally address one another) and no surname. Akhmet joined us in the hotel lobby and greeted us with a little bow and a shy smile. He was tall and slim and even before we heard the name, his features revealed that he was non-European.

During the holiday season, the Intourist agency supplements its regular staff with students of foreign languages: Akhmet was at the Rostov Pedagogical Institute. As he told us later, he would be earning far less than the previous summer, when he had spent his vacation at a Kazakhstan building site and piled up 2,000 roubles for three months' non-stop work (his teacher's starting salary is 135 roubles a month). But this time the work would be more fun and he would have the chance of perfecting his already very good English. By Soviet standards he looked relatively affluent in his smart, navy-blue suit. All Intourist guides are better dressed than the other local people; presumably the agency pays for their clothes and does not rely on Soviet shops.

But even with the best guide, Rostov-on-Don is not a great tourist attraction. It was founded in the mid-eighteenth century as a citadel and market and is still a vital communications centre. The 1914 *Baedeker* observes that, after Kiev and Odessa, it is the best built town in southern Russia but 'offers little of interest to the stranger'. Today, after the wartime destructions, it offers even less. Akhmet took us on a quick drive round the city, gave us the regular tour of the local Chekhov museum, commemorating the cottage where the great writer was born, and then told the chauffeur to drive us to Taganrog on the Azov Sea. 'A pleasant port,' said *Baedeker* – and a very pleasant little port it still remains. .

Even in 1914, only ten years after Anton Chekhov died, the little house had been turned into a place of pilgrimage. The Russians have always revered their literary eminences to a degree unimaginable in the West. An endless stream of placid Soviet citizens in organised groups were being shepherded in and out of the cramped little rooms – which were preserved unchanged, icons and all – while their guides spoke deferentially of the great man and his humble background. The highly individualist and anti-pompous Chekhov must be chuckling in his grave.

Taganrog was unique: in the central town square we saw not the regulation Lenin but a big bronze sculpture of Peter the Great, made by Antokolski in 1903. It was a beautiful day and I asked Akhmet whether we could give the other museums a miss and find a quiet beach. This proved impossible, but he took us to the yacht club and asked us to wait. He came out beaming; we were to be received by the director of the club. Gennady Konstantinovich Cherny was a muscular, handsome man and his whole life was geared to the tremendous job of training the sailing teams for the 1980 Olympics. He gave us some badges commemorating the occasion – in the Soviet Union you can commemorate the future – and marked Tallinn (the capital of Estonia, annexed by the USSR in 1940), which is to be the location of the Olympic sailing events.

Gennady treated us generously to local wine. We drank to the success of our prospective – and respective – teams. Would we like a boat trip round the bay? I felt embarrassed. Having just spent almost a hundred dollars to go to the Askania zoo, I was afraid we could run out of money before getting back to London. How much would it cost? He laughed and said no, he was inviting us to be his guests on the club boat. We gratefully accepted and he telephoned his wife who arrived to join us carrying a hamper of home-made *pirozhki*, little light pastry pasties filled with cabbage and onions or with meat. They were so delicate and delicious that they reminded me of my mother's cooking and were not remotely related to the heavy, greasy objects which carry the same name at the Intourist restaurants and buffets.

We spent one of the happiest hours of our journey in this comfortable and unostentatious motor boat with Gennady as our mentor and a 'captain' at the helm. The white chalk cliffs, climbing steeply from the shore, with clumps of trees, reminded me of the rare sunny days of the south coast at home. We peered into the deep blue sea, which he said had more fish per hectare than any other water in the world (but there was still no fresh fish in the local hotels or shops). We admired the enormous variety and quantity of pleasure boats tied up in the harbour. Gennady said that most of them were built in Poland, and belonged to individuals or clubs. They cost anything from 200 to 100,000 roubles. There are rich people in Russia too, with money to burn.

As a reward for Akhmet's help and kindness I invited him to join us at the theatre. Wherever we went we asked about new films or plays but, until Rostov, nothing contemporary was being performed except war films – and we thought we had had enough reminders of the 'great patriotic war'. At Rostov *Comrade Lyubov* was having its first run. It was a musical version of a straight play about the Civil War, written in 1924, and staged in the theatre attached to the Officers' Club. The play opened with revolutionaries dancing with red ribbons round what looked like a maypole. The play had many laughs at the expense of the officers of the White Army and their camp-followers, strutting their foolish way towards destruction.

The heroine, Comrade Lyubov, is on the Red side and her husband on the White. In the end he recognises his error and commits suicide while the conquering Reds comfort his loyal Bolshevik widow. My favourite character was the elegant countess, who realises that her side has lost and defiantly sings that she will end her days in a Paris brothel. The good and bad were so dramatically opposed that I was reminded of *The Scarlet Pimpernel*, by Baroness Orczy, my favourite book when I was twelve. The only difference was that in her story one's total sympathy was engaged *against* rather than *for* the revolutionaries. As a child I would have been furious with anyone who had tried to persuade me that the crude *tricoteuses* sitting by the guillotine might have had good reason to be angry.

Akhmet thanked me for inviting him but during the show he could not restrain the occasional yawn. I suspect he would have preferred an evening of pop music with Margaret (and so would she). If so, I am sorry. He deserved well of us and I found his status as an Intourist guide highly intriguing.

The Intourist agency is as Russified as most Moscow-controlled institutions. As *Observer* correspondent I had travelled widely in Soviet Asia, visiting Tashkent, Samarkand, Bukhara, Stalinabad (capital of Tadzhikistan which, since I was there, has reverted to its old name of Dashambe), and Alma-Ata. I had seen Asiatics at work and at play. I had been taken to meet native 'ministers of culture' – presumably in the hope that I would interpret their use of their native language as an indication of some degree of independence (which it is not). But everywhere the Moscow-directed apparatus was Russian and the guides were always European.

The 70-kilometre drive to Taganrog gave us time to ask personal questions about one another's background. Akhmet told us he was a Chechen from the Chechen-Ingush ASSR (officially, these letters stand for Autonomous Soviet Socialist Republic, though in reality the area has never been either autonomous or a republic and is no more than a non-self-governing colony). The community to which Akhmet belonged numbered about half a million and was deported with other ethnic groups in 1944. Akhmet said that he was born in Tashkent and his family had returned to their home in the Caucasus when he was one year old. His parents and the rest of the family lived 500 kilometres south-east of Rostov in the very same house from which they had been expelled. He said his people still clung to their old Muslim beliefs and way of life, but he had gone his own way up the educational ladder and had turned his back on religion.

As Akhmet had access only to official Soviet records, he probably knew less than I did about the history of his indomitable people. In the nineteenth century, the Russians had regarded them as wild savages and after the Crimean war they had fled to Turkey. Twenty-five years later they came home, accepting Russian rule. In Stalin's time, after their exile, efforts had been made to regroup them in Uzbekistan, but they insisted on returning to the Caucasus, bringing with them their dead to be reburied.

Just before I left on my tour, a new book, *The Punished Peoples* by Aleksandr M. Nekrich, appeared, giving a well documented account of the whole story of the exile and, in most – though still not all – cases, the return of the millions of Muslims deported from the Crimea and the Caucasus. Nekrich personally witnessed some of the deportations and compiled his history at the Institute of History of the Soviet Academy of Sciences in Moscow. The book was published in the United States after he had left the Soviet Union and became a research fellow at Harvard.

Nekrich claimed that the 1944 deportations had halted the advance of atheism, revived religious fanaticism and fanned anti-Russian and anti-Soviet feelings. Tourists are barred from the regions of the Caucasus where the Muslims predominate but there is plenty of evidence, from Soviet and dissident sources, c f ethnic tension – including occasional outbreaks of violence – between the native communities and the Russian and Ukrainian colonisers.

The Caucasians are only a small minority of the 25–30 million Soviet citizens of Muslim origin (out of the total Soviet population of about 262 million). Are the rest more reconciled to Russian rule? At Zaporozhye, we had met a Jordanian student of civil engineering, Mounir Abu Djieries, who had had the opportunity of visiting the Muslim people in the Tadzhikistan region of Central Asia. Here, too, they seemed to be impervious to the dominant Marxist-Leninist creed. To Mounir himself, communist indoctrination (compulsory in even engineering courses) was water off a duck's back. He said he was in the USSR by order of his king (Hussein of Jordan; most Jordanian students are in Western universities but the King decided to keep fifty in Soviet institutions). Mounir said he had been welcomed by his Muslim co-religionists in Tadzhikistan as a brother and they had told him that they felt closer to Jordan than to Russia. He brought them food and clothing and said that living standards were lower than in Jordan but that educational facilities were better. Senior members of the Muslim communities are now allowed to make their pilgrimages to Mecca and he was conscious of a strong sense of pan-Islamic solidarity.

This is all the more troubling to Moscow. The Asians in the USSR, who retain a Muslim way of life and transnational loyalties, are reproducing much faster than the Europeans, and in the Red Army one conscript in five already comes from communities of Muslim origin. Ethnographers predict that, by the turn of the century, it will be one in three.

We met an Adzhar from Batumi named Khalid, who told the story of his eighteen-year-old cousin, then serving in the Red Army on the Chinese frontier. The boy had got drunk and knifed and killed a fellow soldier. His relatives foregathered as they do in times of trouble, and assigned Khalid, a trained engineer and probably the most articulate member of the clan, to go and rescue the boy from a long gaol sentence or death. Khalid was sent off with several thousand roubles, bottles of cognac, vodka and wine, chicken and geese, boxes of sweets and baskets of fresh fruit.

The soldier was stationed in the mountainous regions of Alma-Ata. Khalid flew, via Tashkent, and called immediately on the Russian commanding officer (he took it for granted that all the officers would be Russian). The retort was bleak: justice would be done. That evening, at his wits' end, Khalid sat in his lodgings – 'a dump that called itself an hotel' – and went into the television room to seek diversion. There, sitting in front of the screen, was this same Russian officer. They started chatting and Khalid invited the officer to his room for drinks. Relations soon warmed up and the Russian asked Khalid what in the world he was doing in this uncivilised place. Khalid reminded him that they had met earlier and retold his story. The officer said that the next evening he would bring along the military procurator (the prosecuting counsel) to see what could be done. Khalid spent a good deal of the next day preparing a real banquet. The two Russians stayed most of the night, eating, exchanging toasts and telling stories. The next morning, haggard and unshaven, the culprit was summoned to the court. He had been deprived of his braces and belt, presumably to prevent suicide. His commanding officer told him he should be beholden to his devoted relations. He would be given a fortnight's leave and would then report for normal duty. The family were overjoyed: the food and drink were all gone but Khalid brought back not only the boy, but all the money.

Looking back on what I saw, heard and read, I feel that Akhmet must have been the exception which proves the rule. There may be a small trickle of Asiatics into the Soviet apparatus but in general the Asiatics and the Europeans distrust each other, they hardly ever intermarry, and the Islamic community, in the Soviet Union as in other parts of the world, is reasserting its identity and rejecting European domination.

Akhmet was not the only reason why our stay in Rostov was rewarding. It was the only city where I knew I would meet residents of British nationality. Richard Bond and Jennifer (Jenny) Thomas were teaching at the university and I had been given their names by their sponsors, the British Council. The Cultural Attaché at the British Embassy in Moscow had cabled them to announce my arrival. Many travelling English deliberately avoid their compatriots but, with some memorable exceptions, I have enjoyed meeting British people living abroad. They are likely not only to welcome a face from home but also to be informative about the local people. Indeed, I regret the old days, when I could have called on a British vice-consul at every stop. According to the 1914 *Baedeker*, a Mr E. Cliveley had even managed to get himself appointed Vice-Consul at charming Taganrog – though he had to double up as Agent for Lloyd's.

Richard and Jenny gave us the warmest of welcomes. We celebrated our meeting by opening the bottle of whisky which I had been treasuring, since I bought it, duty free, on the plane from London. When we went to a restaurant for dinner we had meat kebab (mutton rather than lamb) and raw cherries. For our guests these were rare delicacies as on their regular pay they could not afford hotel meals. Since their arrival, there had been no meat in the shops and the supply of potatoes was irregular. The only time they ate well was when they were invited to the homes of some of their wealthier students. They were both left-wingers and their trade union in London would have been shocked by the conditions and pay (when their electric bulbs fused the college could not replace them). Yet they were enjoying themselves hugely and both had applied for another year's assignment to a Soviet university.

One advantage of teaching in a Soviet rather than a British university is that Russian students work harder. To the average Russian, university education is a valued privilege. Further, the Russians are natural readers: the demand for serious books, whether classic or modern, is infinitely higher than in the United States or Western Europe. Russian intellectuals were furious when the Soviet authorities allowed the publication of only ten thousand copies of the formerly banned Russian poet, Mandelshtam (1876–1944). His poetry is difficult and austere yet a Russian assured me that a million copies could easily have been sold.

What can the young Russian learn about the outside world? The Soviet authorities have gone to great lengths to ensure that a small and selected number have specialised knowledge of foreign languages. They have set up schools in which all the lessons are given in English or, less often, in German or French. But the high linguistic standards attained in these schools (accessible mainly to the children of well connected parents) are not complemented by any instruction about life and thought in the countries where these languages are spoken. Apart from the Communist press, which they might as well read in their own language, their access to Western publications is very limited and even those newspapers which they sometimes see are first carefully expurgated.

Though many contemporary writers are translated and published (they include Evelyn Waugh, Graham Greene, Iris Murdoch, Margaret Drabble, John le Carré, Michael Frayn and, most surprising of all, John Updike), these works come out in small numbers and are snatched up long before the ordinary student can get to them. An unusually large edition of 150,000 copies of Evelyn Waugh's *Brideshead Revisited* sold out in three days: a million could have been sold in a week.

But, although the Soviet Union signed the world Copyright Convention in May 1973, which lays down that works cannot be abridged without the author's explicit consent, they have never hesitated to make changes appropriate to their own sexual and social mores.

The written word, in this century as in the last, has been

more important in Russia and Eastern Europe than in the West. And, battered by the ideological assault from the libertarian world, the Communists, like their Tsarist predecessors, tend to panic. This is what seems to have happened over the translation of Heinrich Böll's novel *Gruppenbild mit Dame*, after the author had said the Soviet adaptation made a mockery of the original narrative and characterisation. The dispute was taken further by an American Germanist, Henry Glade, who examined the translation in collaboration with a Soviet writer, Konstantin Bogatyerev, well known for his translations of Rilke. Their joint study of the way the work had been tampered with was the subject of an article entitled 'The translator as a censor', published by the University of Dayton. A few days after it appeared, 51-year-old Bogatyrev was found near his home in Moscow, lying in a pool of blood, with his skull broken by some heavy metal object. There were no signs of robbery: his money and belongings were untouched. He was buried near Pasternak's grave in Peredelkino, and those unorthodox writers who dared attend the funeral are convinced he was the victim of the KGB summary justice.

The students in Rostov had to rely for their knowledge of contemporary Britain not on contemporary British writers but on a Soviet text book, entitled: *England: History, Geography and Culture*, printed in Kiev in 1976. The author asserts that although the British Empire is 'in decline', its colonies are still exploited and they remain 'Britain's appendages for raw materials'.

On English culture, T. S. Eliot is recognised as creator of the modern school of poetry, and is said to have turned towards Catholicism (in fact, he went no further than High Church Anglicanism) 'in order to help curb the disobedient masses'. As for James Joyce, he is accused of 'using classical allusions and polyglot quotations' in order to serve 'undemocratic purposes'. The textbook ends, however, on a cheering note. 'With the Communists as their nucleus', the left-wing forces 'are leading Britain towards Socialism.'

Given this level of 'History, Geography and Culture', the Soviet student cannot be expected to know much about the outside world. The more inquiring ones tune in to foreign radio stations. But, in some cases, the ignorance is alarming. Could a student of *journalism* at the University of Rostov really believe, as I was assured, that, in their religious rites, Baptists kill babies? I wanted to check for myself. Richard gave a little party for his students in his small bed-sitter, borrowing extra chairs from the nearby rooms. The boys and girls at the gathering represented an astonishing spread: one came from Sakhalin on the Pacific, another from the West Ukraine, one from the Crimea, another from Leningrad. The Soviet authorities evidently encourage mobility. One guest was a French instructor, shrewd and cynical, who had been in Rostov for several years.

The deluded student was Nyura, an attractive and well-dressed brunette of Armenian origin. She lived with her family in Rostov's Armenian district.

Chatting about local life, I threw in a question: were the Baptists holding an international conference at Rostov? Nyura rose to the bait and said that such a conference had been planned, but fortunately the police had forbidden it having discovered that the Baptist religion requires the sacrifice of babies. 'Nyura, don't be so naive and ridiculous!' said the Frenchman.

I said I knew all about Baptists (an exaggeration) and human sacrifice would be at variance with all their beliefs. Nyura screwed up her pretty face and said she must be thinking of another sect. 'Perhaps you were told this terrible lie about the Jews?' I said, remembering that for generations anti-Semites have peddled the story that Jews kill babies for the feast of Passover. No, she said, not the Jews! When we left, she was still groping to remember which religion it could be.

We discussed the University courses and I asked the students how they could possibly study atheism (compulsory for everybody) without reading the Bible and knowing what they were supposed to disbelieve? They said that their textbooks provided them with appropriate extracts. Nyura commented: 'There are still some families who believe in God and practise religion so the Party cannot allow the import and free distribution of bibles. But when everyone is atheist, there will be no restrictions. You will be able to bring in as many bibles as you like!'

The most intelligent of the students was Genya, who was soon to leave to join his wife in East Germany. Genya and I shared a special interest in Comecon, the Communist economic bloc, which includes the Soviet Union, Poland, Czechoslovakia, Hungary, Rumania, Bulgaria, East Germany, Cuba, Mongolia and Vietnam. He was writing a thesis on Comecon and I told him of my journey round all the European capitals earlier in the year.

My articles on Comecon had been confiscated at the frontier, and he regretted that he could not read them. When we came back through Rostov, I invited Genya to join Richard and Jenny as our guests at the Intourist restaurant. It was a rewarding encounter. Genya, who was an economics graduate, agreed with me that the economic integration of the Comecon group would depend on the elaboration of a single economic plan so that there could be a division of labour between the member states. If they went on, as at present, each having its own national plan, they were bound to compete against each other in trying to produce the kind of commodities which they could sell for hard currency on world markets. Genya conceded that the elaboration of a single economic plan might take a very long time; but he thought 'objectively' (a favourite word of his) that such a plan was in the logic of history.

As I saw it, 'the logic of history' pointed the other way. Whatever the economic arguments, politics will always impede agreement on a single Comecon economic plan. The smaller member states are too afraid of being sucked into the giant Soviet economic machine. And as one Comecon country has an economy (not to mention an army) far bigger than all the others put together, an equal partnership is impossible. Genya gave me his future address in Leipzig and we agreed we would continue the argument the next time I visited Eastern Germany. At Rostov it was from my academic contacts that we had benefited. At Krasnodar, our next stop, we had equally good luck with Margaret's. She had spent a month attending a Russian course at Krasnodar University, sensibly choosing a city off the tourist circuit. She had enjoyed it enormously and longed to be back.

12

Krasnodar: Happy Families

'Why don't you Westerners ever write about a happy Soviet family?' Boris, a biology lecturer at Krasnodar University, put the question with a grin. I resolved to take up the challenge.

There could be no better place than Krasnodar from which to take a closer look at the cheerful side of Soviet life. We had left Rostov in pelting rain. As we drove into the Kuban valley the sun came out over a vast expanse of sunflowers. The golden image was added to by fields of ripening grain. The previous crop of one of the richest regions of the Soviet Union had beaten all records. Krasnodar received a special message of congratulations from Comrade Brezhnev. Posters were urging the workers to respond by doing even better this year.

'Think how rich we would be if it wasn't all carted off to Moscow!' observed a local, as we studied the impressive upward graph of production, framed outside the Party headquarters. He was being a little unfair: Moscow pays much more than in the past. The low price of bread is irrelevant: the government policy is to keep bread cheap and subsidise grain.

The friendlier atmosphere was apparent even before we reached the city. On the outskirts we saw the usual exhortations, Brezhnev's 'visual aids': 'Communism will triumph!', 'The Plan is the Law: We shall fulfil it!' and, over a vast mural of brawny boys and girls, 'Our young people are ceaselessly at work!' (not altogether my impression).

But the Party here was also offering some personal advice:

'Don't exceed the speed limit!' (90 kmph for cars, 60 kmph for trucks, but vehicles which are capable of moving faster generally do). And, boldly displayed, along the side of a bridge crossing the road: 'Happy Journey!'

Our friend Boris has never joined the Communist Party and he does not have to dedicate his very limited free time to Party jobs. One dissident who used to be a Party member but left in 1969 recalls that, before going, he had been expected to do twenty-seven regular jobs for the Party and hardly ever had an evening to himself.

As a lecturer in a small but agreeable university, Boris feels that he does not do too badly. His demands are modest: there is no fresh meat but enough protein in sausages, eggs and cheese. He and Irene, his wife, are in their early thirties but the diet makes it hard to retain youthful figures. He pays only a peppercorn rent for a newly acquired three-room flat which houses six members of the family. He spends about 4 per cent of his income keeping his little boy at the local kindergarten (15 roubles a term). Boris earns 135 roubles a month, which is less than the average manual worker, but his wife also works at the university and between them they can afford a good hi-fi, radio, colour TV and a washing-machine.

They admitted that things are a little provincial and that sometimes they sigh for Leningrad, where she had studied. But they feel that Leningrad is far more accessible to them than Moscow was to Chekhov's Three Sisters.

Krasnodar has little cultural life and the local theatre company was wound up a couple of years ago after a 'skandal' which rocked the city's intelligentsia. According to the former director of the theatre, the leading lady had an affair with an actor and was subsequently told she had contracted VD. She plotted a memorable revenge. All the players were invited to a drinks party and each one was given an intimate personal embrace. She played her part magnificently and it was only after the party was over that the victims discovered why it had been held. The director was dismissed and the company scattered.

Though never a Party member, Boris has no objection to being called out occasionally by the Party for a day's 'voluntary' manual labour. Far from feeling humiliated, he enjoys these collective outings. Recently, the university staff spent a Saturday working on the local sunflower plantation. The seeds had been sown too closely together and the academic teams, men and women together working in rows, plucked by hand every alternate flower. The mind boggles at the thought of a senior common room of a British university so engaged.

Boris's father is also at the university: a full professor and a much-respected teacher. Students, he says, should be treated not as empty pots into which to pour information but rather as torches which need illuminating. He supplements his salary by writing textbooks and can afford a small car. Also, with Boris's help he has built himself a dacha – a country cottage – on the mountain slopes overlooking the Black Sea. It has electricity but no plumbing. The family pride is the orchard. When the cherry tree is in bloom, Boris's mother stays at the house so that, in case of frost, she can keep the buds warm with bonfires. During the night she sets the alarm clock to awaken her every two hours to stoke the flames.

Boris is an only son and the family clings closely together. He and the children have constant access to the car and dacha. When he and Irene are busy, the grandparents take the children. Their standards are somewhat Victorian. He deplores any manifestations of the permissive society, and favours hard work, obedience to parental authority, conventional attire and marital fidelity. He knows that divorces in the Soviet Union have increased vastly but says that 'in his circle' a very poor view is taken of any man or woman who deserts the family.

Generally, in the Soviet Union, the family remains closely knit. The Brezhnev 1977 Constitution makes parents responsible for the education and conduct of their children and also requires those of working age to look after retired relatives. The Soviet pension, a maximum of 80 roubles a month, is too low to live on and is calculated on the assumption that pensioners will live with their families. Even lower pensions are paid to those who stayed in the cities under German occupation and can therefore be suspected of having collaborated. In Kiev, where the Germans remained for three years, the wives of many soldiers stayed at home. Fortunately no records were kept at Krasnodar, which was occupied for only six months.

The 'family' was the theme of the film *The Cranes in the Sky*, which we saw on our first evening in Krasnodar, our first chance to see any contemporary performances. Apart from the musical comedy about the civil war at Rostov, Intourist had nothing to suggest but circuses, films about the war, or revivals of the classics. The new film was remarkably well acted, sentimental, funny and mercifully free of politics. The story was simple: a blonde of Rubenesque proportions has deserted her clownishly innocent lorry-driving husband. He sinks into melancholy and his family decide he needs another woman. We see several shots of would-be brides – evidently victims of the perennial housing shortage – who cast an envious eye on his simple cottage. He refuses them all. His loneliness ends one night when he finds, at the back of his lorry, a little boy who has escaped from the local orphanage. A friendly local policeman warns that only married couples may legally adopt children. Luckily, the man rediscovers his wife, who is being brutally maltreated by her lover. The boy reconciles them in the best Shirley Temple tradition.

The next morning, while Margaret was visiting former colleagues, I relaxed in the sunshine at the edge of a pool in a beautifully tended garden which stretched right through the middle of the town's main boulevard – fountains, roses, shrubberies and clumps of lime and cypress trees. Term was ending and cheerful students were coming out of an institute opposite the hotel. The girls were on high heels or platform shoes and some wore fashionable blonde wigs. Most of the boys wore bright-coloured shirts. It was an atmosphere of well-being, animation and goodwill.

So why not follow Boris's advice, stop being critical and think about happy Soviet families? I opened my newspaper, the *Komsomolets Kubani* (Komsomol Member of the Kuban Region). *Pravda* and *Izvestia* had been sold out before I got up and the only daily on sale was this local newspaper. Its masthead carried the famous device 'Workers of the World Unite!' and most of the articles were domestic and predictable. But there was a front-page story, datelined London. The main head was 'The Face of the "Free" World', with the subhead 'The tragedy of the unemployed'. The article began with the account of the suicide of an English school-leaver, driven to desperation by his failure to find a job. It carried statistics on the growth of unemployment among young Britishers with comments from Western sources. There was no mention of the fact that many young people live on social security while they look for the kind of job they want. This would be hard even to imagine in the Soviet Union, where no work means no pay. If there is no suitable job, you take an unsuitable one. In Rostov, women who had graduated in psychology were employed as auxiliary nurses. The planners had overestimated their needs for psychologists, so the graduates were redeployed.

The article ended with an extract from a report by the Cambridge School of Applied Economics, forecasting that, if present policies continued, there would soon be four million British unemployed. The Cambridge School has long been considered the economists' Cassandra and, like Cassandra, they may in the end prove right. But a more balanced report might have referred to other less gloomy official and unofficial forecasts. But why be balanced? The Krasnodar paper needed to demonstrate the superiority of the Soviet over the British system and to encourage Komsomol members to read about suicidal British youth and say to themselves, 'There – but for the grace of the Communist Party – go I.'

But the outside world is not entirely excluded. Boris and his friends listen regularly to the BBC, which they think is more reliable than Soviet stations. He wishes there were more broadcasts about the British way of life. He regrets the BBC concentration on dissidents and Jews.

In Krasnodar, he claims, the Jews occupy relatively senior posts in the university. But he thought it better that I should not try to meet them. The Carter human rights campaign worries him as a potential threat to détente which, to him, means easier access for the Russians to the people and literature of the outside world. Boris favours détente the way a practising churchman favours virtue. Oddly, he accepts the officially inspired reports that the Radio Liberty emigrés are a discreditable bunch. If he met them he might find they shared similar values. Anatoli Kuznetsov told me that he decided to quit Russia when the KGB began insisting he should inform on the activities of his friend, the poet Yevtushenko. Boris would never be a police spy. But then he is not a Party man and does not meet the kind of people who interest the police.

The degree of Soviet isolation was brought home forcibly at Krasnodar's new 'House of Books' – a shop stretching over about 100 metres in the centre of town. Its spaciousness, clearly marked sections and excellent lighting put to shame London's famous Foyle's, Dillon's or Hatchard's. What was harrowing was the paucity and narrowness of choice of the books available on its half-empty shelves. Only some well illustrated children's books and the map section seemed to have escaped the Party's heavy hand. We managed to buy a useful Soviet road atlas, the kind of publication which disappears almost as soon as it comes out.

The second-hand section specialises in leather-bound editions of Lenin's complete works. The works of most of the other old Bolsheviks disappeared when they did, during the purge. The more interesting second-hand books go into the private network in Leningrad and Moscow. One Krasnodar collector told us that he had found a copy of the 1914 Russian *Baedeker* ten years earlier in a Leningrad *bouquiniste* for only 8 roubles. I had searched for it in vain all over London. The collector was not a rich man but he said he would not part with it at any price. His most cherished acquisition was the complete works of Conan Doyle in eight volumes. A few years previously he had paid 20 roubles for it and now, he said, it would fetch 150. The rocketing price can be attributed partly to inflation. Despite efforts to fix prices, the purchasing power of the rouble is falling, though not as fast as that of the dollar or the pound. A Soviet economics journal early in 1979 conceded that, both in the current Five Year Plan and in the previous one, wages have been rising faster than supplies; in other words the Russians are suffering from the familiar inflationary pattern – too much money chasing too few goods.

But the increased price of English books also reflects a steadily increasing demand. And, though Russians may not be able to cope with the more obscure twentieth-century writers (supposing they can get them), Conan Doyle is easy, fun, written in good plain English and ideologically unobjectionable.

It was in the legal section of the Krasnodar House of Books that I thought I had stumbled on a study of the human rights of the Soviet citizen against the state. I purchased it and brought it home for expert advice. It is published by the University of Saratov and the foreword states that it is aimed primarily at teachers and students in law schools but can also be used for education and propaganda purposes. The chapters deal with various branches of the Soviet administration: the economy, education, health, sciences, culture, public order, and even the status of Soviet citizens in foreign countries.

What then are the rights of Boris and his family as they struggle with the huge bureaucracy which organises every department of their lives? In the international arena, the Soviet Government claims that the rights of their own citizens, including the right to work and the right to housing, mean far more to ordinary people than the rights of political dissent, about which the West fusses so much. These, they claim, affect only a sprinkling of disgruntled intellectuals.

Did my textbook sustain this thesis? I consulted an eminent specialist, Ivo Lapenna, the Professor of Soviet and East-European law at the London School of Economics, formerly Professor of International Law at Zagreb. The Professor is not committedly anti-Soviet. He has been to the Soviet Union and been favourably impressed by some Soviet initiatives and by the work of some of the Russian procurators – those dual-purpose officials, inherited from the past, who act as both guardians of the law and as public prosecutors. He considers that the Russians are doing useful work, notably on problems of juvenile delinquency.

In Professor Lapenna's view, my book only confirmed the fundamental reality about the Russian system, as valid today as it was in Tsarist times: the interests of the private individual and the interests of the state are deemed to be one and the same thing. In other words, the citizens cannot have rights against the state. The only change is that in the old days the state was incarnated in the Tsar and now it is incarnated in the Communist Party – in practice the Party leaders.

The Professor pointed out to me that I had mistranslated

the title of the book, which was part of the reason why it had so intrigued me. I had understood it to mean: 'The legal *rights* (my italics) of the citizens in relation to the branches of the state administration'. The subject was not their legal rights but their legal 'position'.

As long as Boris and his family do nothing to offend the Party, he has a reasonable chance (which, particularly in medical cases, can be improved by well-directed payments to the appropriate people) of securing all the benefits to which they are entitled. If a junior bureaucrat denies him his claim, he can take the matter up with the man's superior. If that fails, he can go to the spacious offices of the revered, beribboned and uniformed procurator. The procurator's office functions at four levels: district, regional, union republic and USSR. Appeals can be taken all the way up. But at the top of the two pyramids – of the administration and of the procurator's office – is the Communist Party leadership.

The task of ombudsman is carried out not only by the procurator's office but also in the columns of newspapers and journals. If Boris feels he has been unfairly treated, he can write and complain to the local or national press. But it would be sensible, before writing, to make sure that his gripe fits into the current Party line. Campaigns of utmost severity are often officially launched against bureaucratic or economic mismanagement; they name specific offenders, and letters can be grist to the mill. On the other hand, if a letter strikes an individualist note, the writer might find himself damagingly labelled as a troublemaker.

Boris and his academic colleagues must be particularly careful to avoid blotting their copy-book, for in the university world there is no security of tenure. Academic appointments are renewed every five years and a party-dominated staff committee decides whether a man should be reappointed to the same job, sacked or promoted.

Boris does not need a law book to tell him he is not allowed to consort with dissidents or to organise political meetings and demonstrations. Officially there are no political prisoners in the Soviet Union. But what is 'political'? A section of the Soviet criminal code under which many people have been successfully prosecuted imposes prison sentences for 'activities against the State'. Opposing Communist rule today is just as illegal as, in the old days, it would have been to oppose the Tsar – although, as Roy Medvedev writes in *On Social Democracy*, the new technologies of counter-espionage make conspiracy a lot harder now than it was in Lenin's day.

If the Party wants someone 'inside', there is no difficulty in discovering an appropriate article of the criminal code under which he can be gaoled. Even private conversations, as I later learnt first-hand from the KGB, can be interpreted as 'anti-Soviet agitation and propaganda': maximum penalty seven years' hard labour. The are also laws against 'hooliganism' and it is a commonplace for KGB thugs to beat up a culprit and, when he defends himself, have him arrested for disturbing public order. Then there is 'parasitism', that is to say failure to earn your living and therefore living off others. In some cases Jews who have asked to emigrate are dismissed, refused any other job (the only employer is the state), and then punished as parasites.

And there are still the exceptional cases, such as the assassination of the translator Konstantin Bogatyerev, where a person can be rubbed out, no questions asked.

Would the Soviet Union be run more rationally and less harshly if women rather than men were in charge? My legal textbook had nothing on women's rights as, in principle, there is full sexual equality. But principle is one thing and practice another. The males dominate every institution from the Politburo down to the smallest factory or farm. There is no discrimination in wage rates. They are fixed in Moscow, for the whole country and for both sexes. Irene is academically senior to Boris and earns 20 roubles a month more than he does. But she would have to be exceptional to qualify for a professorship and has hardly any chance of heading a university or an institute.

Although there is equal pay for equal work, the men keep the high-grade and best paid jobs for themselves. In the sixty years of emancipation, remarkably little has changed.

Warning of roadworks ahead are signalled in the Soviet Union, as elsewhere, by the familiar picture of a man with a shovel. But when we reached the location the shovels were always wielded by women, mostly wearing felt slippers and shawls. The men sat at the machines – steam-rollers, bulldozers and tractors – and gave the orders. Along the roads, women operate the trolley-buses and trams but the men drive the self-propelled buses (a job which sometimes earns them 300 roubles a month – nearly twice what Boris earns). The men drive the trains; the women repair the rails.

Almost all the private cars are driven by men. 'Where is your chauffeur?' was the first question put to us wherever we arrived. Margaret was exasperated by the exclamations of surprise greeting the news that she herself was our driver. Once, while she was washing the car, some laundry-women shouted at her that she should not be doing a man's job.

Customs change slowly and women's lib has not yet caught on. Men are in short supply and, having chosen a wife, they expect to be looked after. The women thus combine full-time jobs with bringing up families, cleaning the house, standing in queues and very often sharing the kitchen with others. No wonder they employ go-slow tactics in their reproductive tasks. Among the European ethnic groups big families are a rarity, even though women with ten children still qualify for the title 'Heroine of the Soviet Union'.

'What birth-control methods do you use?' I asked a group of girl students. The answer is that the pill is not generally available, it can be obtained only in the main cities, and legally only on prescription. For the many who cannot afford to buy contraceptive devices on the black market, there are the traditional methods – the 'safe' period and abortions.

Our itinerary allowed three days at Krasnodar because I had thought I could use it as a base from which to visit the Pepsi-Cola plant. Novorossiysk has no sleeping accommodation for foreigners but it lies on the road open to tourists and is only two and a half hours' drive away. So would Intourist please inform the management that I was coming? No, they would not. They made inquiries and were told I could not go.

13
Novorossiysk: Pepsi-colonisation

Andrei Rubinovich Oganov, the Armenian boss of the Pepsi bottling plant at Novorossiysk, gave us a cordial welcome. And the moral of *that* is that when dealing with Soviet officialdom never take no for an answer.

It was certainly not the fault of dear, plump Emma, the Intourist manageress at Krasnodar. She did her best. Among other things, she extricated us from a dingy, cramped motel, into which we had been mistakenly booked. At the reception desk at the best hotel, the Kavkaz, we were told that as we were driving ourselves we could not qualify for the *de luxe* category. The written evidence that I had paid *de luxe* rates and the information that I had stayed in *de luxe* rooms in all the previous hotels failed to shake the stubborn receptionist.

I demanded to see the manageress and, after one uncomfortable night, Emma had us moved from the motel to the Kavkaz. It was to her that I entrusted my letter of introduction to the local Pepsi people with the request that she should arrange my visit. She made numerous phone calls, as I well remember because, while she was waiting, she insisted that I share some of the delicious but over-rich birthday cake passed around by a younger member of the manifestly overstaffed office.

My heart sank when she said that the head of the regional breweries, responsible for the Pepsi plant, said that my visit would have to be cleared through Moscow. Emma suggested that I should come back in a few hours but I knew the answer would be 'nyet'. On my return she gave three reasons why the visit was impossible. First, Moscow had not been told. Emma said they had recently been visited by a Pepsi Vice-President, Herbert Ley, a visit that had been arranged a long time in advance by the Company Chairman, Donald Kendall. But Donald Kendall knew about my visit, I said, and the Pepsi letter of introduction had been issued on his instructions. Indeed, his marketing director for Eastern Europe, Mr Klaus Schertling, had given me more than I asked for: besides the letter signed by himself and another Pepsi executive at the Vienna headquarters, I came away with Pepsi pendants, Pepsi scarves and a whole box of bright blue cigarette lighters carrying the name 'Pepsi' in red Russian characters, which came in very useful for tips.

Klaus Schertling had even gone beyond the call of duty. Hearing that, despite repeated requests, Avis had not provided us with a spare petrol can, he left us his own. We found it waiting for us in our Vienna hotel with a note: 'So that you may not wind up high and dry'. Contrary to some dire predictions, we never did. There were times, however, when only low-grade fuel was available at the Soviet petrol pumps and the Volkswagen went more smoothly after we topped up their crude mix with high-quality reserve we had brought along in Schertling's can.

Emma's second point was that the Pepsi premises were being cleaned, or, as she put it, having their 'sanitary day', the plant would therefore not be in production. Unlike Western managers, the Soviets seem to think that cleaning and operating an installation cannot proceed simultaneously. I was reminded of a chilling experience earlier in the year when I was staying at my favourite Moscow hotel, the National. It was a cold, snowy night and yet all the clients had to eat out. No food would be served either in the restaurants or in the private rooms. Why? 'The National is having a sanitary day.'

Never mind, I would be sorry not to see the bottling process but it was not essential. The Vienna office had shown me pictures of the girls in overalls. I do not understand machinery and a factory floor is an unsuitable place for conversation. I still wanted to visit the premises and meet the manager.

At this point, Emma told a fib, though I never found out whether she was conveying someone else's misinformation or whether she invented it herself to justify the refusal. The interruption of work for sanitary purposes was being used she said as an opportunity to install new machinery. The plant was therefore closed. When we arrived we found the plant open and the Pepsi people later told me they had no plans for installing new machines.

But poor Emma could hardly be expected to overrule Moscow. So I retrieved my letter of introduction, rested at Krasnodar for an extra day and left for Novorossiysk at 7 a.m. on the day we were due in Sochi. We had to pass through the city anyway on our arduous 436-kilometre journey south.

By 9.30 a.m. we had parked the car in the Novorossiysk central parking space and were walking through the open market. A few bottles of Pepsi were on sale at one of the peasant stalls and going for only a few kopecks above the official price. Like all other manufactured commodities on sale in the Soviet Union, Pepsi is priced in Moscow (which fixes some twelve million prices a year). The prices have very little connexion with the costs of production; they are designed to direct demand, rather than to respond to it.

On the unofficial market, however, Pepsi has a considerable scarcity value and the price we saw in the market was uncommonly low. A man at Yalta had told me that he travelled in a Pepsi van all the way from Yevpatoria to Moscow, 1,500 kilometres away, and the driver stopped several times along the way, unloading crates at 1·50 roubles a bottle – five times the official figure. In comparison with Soviet drinks, even at the official rate, Pepsi is dear – twice as expensive as Soviet produced fruit juices and four times as much as the traditional kvass, made from fermented black bread and sold on tap in most Soviet cities, from huge mobile barrels.

Just outside the open market we hailed a local taxi and asked to be taken to the Pepsi-cola bottling plant.

The driver knew precisely where to go but he was a dour man and the only one on our journey who refused a tip. He had a highly adverse view of Pepsi-cola, saying that it was unhealthy and caused swellings of children's eyes. But he delivered us and waited to take us back. Presumably he could comfort himself with the slogan 'Communism will prevail', displayed over the top of the Pepsi plant (perhaps to prevent it from appearing as a temple to capitalist achievement). The spectacle would have saddened Kendall, who, only a few months previously, had claimed that East–West trade would 'improve a network of interlocking relations of mutual values'. What values?

We handed round cigarettes at the porter's lodge and within three minutes were shown into Oganov's office. He peered, a little suspiciously, at Schertling's letter, probably unable to read English but certainly recognising the Pepsi letterhead, and then invited us to come in for a chat. The choice was Pepsi or beer, both produced in his factory. He apologised that production was suspended while the place was being cleaned, which he said happened every month, but he assured us that everything was going very well indeed.

I did not ask him why, as I had heard from the Pepsi engineers, the Russians only used their plant at 60 per cent of its capacity. Technical hitches such as failure of transport, shortage of bottles and unavailability of workers waste about one-third of the potential working-time.

Oganov asked whether we knew that the Pepsi concentrate comes from our own country. Geographically, he was not far wrong. Syrup is manufactured in the Irish Republic, where labour is cheaper. The Irish will be sorry to hear that the grand story of their independence has not yet reached Novorossiysk. Oganov also asked if I knew where the raw material came from. I had to admit ignorance: Pepsi keeps its secrets to itself.

I had arrived in the Soviet Union with the innocent notion that the Russians must be encouraging Pepsi as an alternative to alcohol – of which consumption is increasing at a frightening rate. A Krasnodar friend had disabused me: Sibirskaya was the brand of vodka with which Pepsi should be mixed. Was this true? Oganov laughed. No! Pepsi is excellent with any vodka.

Oganov brought out his leather-bound photograph album and we were invited to admire pictures of the launching party, in which President Brezhnev, Chairman Kendall and he walked side by side in the factory grounds. We drank toasts to détente and to East–West collaboration. But Oganov made it clear that President Carter had disappointed him – a sentiment he no doubt shared with Kendall, who is an old friend of former President Nixon. When the original deal was signed it was assumed that the Americans would soon extend the 'most favoured nation' treatment (tariff preference) to the Russians. This was prevented by the Democrats' human rights campaign and the Zionist lobby. Oganov did not mention the reasons but he considered it outrageous that Pepsi came into the Soviet Union without any customs whereas there were heavy taxes on the Stolichnaya vodka and Georgian champagne for which it was exchanged.

Not that the Americans seemed to be doing badly. The Soviet alcoholic drinks are marketed in the US on behalf of Pepsi by the Monsieur Henri Wine Company, which in 1978 grossed nearly $20 million. Oganov had cause to deplore the worsening of East–West relations but was it exclusively the Americans' fault? Oganov (who, as the Pepsi people told me, belonged to the hierarchy of the Party, not to the management) would allow no aspersions on Soviet foreign policy. 'We must never forget that our government has given this country the longest period of peace in its history.' He was right.

The new bottling plant at Yevpatoria had only recently been opened. A young Russian on the Yalta beach had said that Novorossiysk Pepsi was far better than the local brew. Could this be true? Yes, said Oganov. Perhaps it was because Novorossiysk is so careful about its sanitation. The Pepsi people later insisted that Pepsi was the same wherever it was produced.

But later, a British visitor to Moscow said that he had tasted Pepsi there (no indication of where it was bottled) and it left a black coating in his mouth.

Novorossiysk was the launching-pad for a bold programme for the Pepsi-colonisation of the entire country. In 1978 Kendall signed an agreement to double the number of plants from five to ten. The Pepsi empire, by the mid-1980s, will stretch from the Baltic to Siberia and from Leningrad and Tallinn to Georgia and Central Asia. It is too soon to say whether Pepsi will be upstaged by their traditional rival Coca-Cola, which has expansionist ambitions in China.

At the time of the new Pepsi deal, the East-European Bulletin of the American consultancy, *Business International*, said, 'The Pepsi strategy is now emerging as an almost classical approach for selling consumer goods in Eastern Europe.' The Bulletin then listed five key elements which contributed to this result. The first was perseverance. Yes indeed, anyone liable to discouragement or depression should not do business with the Soviet Union – nor spend their holidays there.

The second, expressed in consultancy jargon, was 'up-front investment in market development'. Not that Pepsi needed any advertising to capture the Soviet consumers. Demand is always ahead of supply. The problem was to induce Soviet officials to include Pepsi in their economic plan. The fight for official backing goes back to 1959, the year of the American Exhibition in Moscow, where the then Vice-President Richard Nixon had a televised quarrel in a model American kitchen with Chairman Khrushchev. On that occasion, Kendall induced Khrushchev to drink a glass of Pepsi (history does not record whether it was laced with vodka) and fifteen years later the first bottling plant went into production. Meanwhile, Pepsi had spent an estimated $50,000 annually exhibiting at the Leipzig Fair – the meeting-place between Western businessmen and Communist planners.

The third 'key element' was 'the use of familiar faces in negotiations'. Kendall and his Vice-President Ley were by now well-know figures in Moscow. At the height of the détente in 1974 Kendall took the unusual step of increasing the Soviet familiarisation with his company by holding an annual meeting of his board of directors at a Soviet Black Sea resort.

The fourth item was 'quality control'. The company regularly sends representatives to the Soviet Union and samples of the locally bottled Pepsi are tested in West-German laboratories. As I mentioned, there is conflicting evidence about the quality of Soviet-produced Pepsi. But the company is plainly doing its best.

Fifth, Pepsi accepts what the Bulletin calls 'counter-trade' – in other words a barter of goods rather than an exchange of cash. One litre of vodka is valued at one litre of Pepsi concentrate. The Soviet planners only part with gold or convertible currency to buy what they really need: grain or technology.

Though Kendall is certainly a pioneer in selling consumer products to the Russians, their favourite American businessman – whose projects run into billions rather than millions of dollars – is the aged tycoon, Dr Armand Hammer, of Occidental Petroleum. He was a personal friend of Lenin and is the only foreigner allowed to fly unaccompanied by Soviet pilots in and out of Soviet airfields. Other big operators are also allowed to bring in their own executive jets, but they are required to have Soviet pilots on board. Though Hammer is well into his eighties, he frequently pops over to Moscow to maintain his personal contacts and retain supervision over his multiple interests on Soviet territory. Before leaving London I phoned Dr Hammer, who was on his way from Moscow back to his Californian home, and he told me that he had just persuaded the Russians to let him build a golf course. I said that I had met his people in Moscow earlier in the year and was much impressed by – and hoped to write about – his many grandiose projects. He said he would be happy to help me.

Unfortunately, our route did not go through Odessa, where Occidental Petroleum have a fertiliser plant – another case of 'counter-trade' in which the Americans supply sulphuric acid and the Russians ammonia, potash and urea. But I did manage to find out something about the workings of the plant as I ran into Pete Cimino, the American manager who happened to be staying in the same hotel when we reached Tbilisi.

Cimino was a quick-witted, temperamental little man, proud of having remained friendly with the local personnel while at the same time forcing them to work fast enough to export a first ship-load from Odessa in July, a month after we left. Though I did not realise it at the time, the date was vital: Hammer was coming for the opening ceremony and would then spend a few days with President Brezhnev at the Soviet leader's holiday home in the Crimea. Pictures of the two old men in shirt-sleeves were published in both Russian and American newspapers.

For Cimino, as for most businessmen working in the Soviet

Union, manpower shortage was the real headache. Party officials could help. For this reason Westerners prefer to deal directly with Party people – like our friend Oganov – rather than with technicians or managers. Cimino got his building completed only because the local labour-force was supplemented from two outside sources: the clerical staff combed from administrative offices in Odessa (the Soviet Union does not share Western objections to using women for construction jobs) and conscripts sent in by the Red Army. One reason why the Soviet Union keeps so many men under arms may be that they provide an invaluable and disciplined labour force, urgently needed not only in the construction industry but, as we saw, for harvesting and road repairs.

The housing shortage at Odessa was overcome by lodging some of the extra labour force in ships anchored in the port. Cimino's principal difficulty was to find qualified men, particularly chemical engineers and foundrymen. The Soviet authorities would not provide visas for American or British specialists, and from their point of view this makes sense. They do not have the organisational skills to extract maximum benefit from high-cost labour. In one plant in the Ukraine twenty-five American technicians had been brought in and housed 40 kilometres away from their job. Day after day they were left stranded in their hostel when, without explanation, their buses or their interpreters failed to turn up.

The Soviet specialists sent to Cimino were so far below American standards of proficiency that he had to set up his own training school – hoping that, once trained, the men would stay. According to one Western businessman, a typical Soviet engineer has qualifications obtainable at an American high school. The title 'engineer' covers mechanics trained in particular specialities – sewerage, transport, ventilation, etc. – so that twenty 'engineers' are needed on a project where, in the West, one would do.

Travellers who are sensibly sceptical about official visits to factories or farms can get more reliable information from the Western technicians employed in the Soviet Union, of whom there are now between seven and eight thousand. One of the most surprising things I learned was that Soviet labour is very mobile. Except within the defence industries, people are always changing jobs. Wage scales are fixed in Moscow but there is nothing to prevent someone leaving one kind of work if he finds something better paid elsewhere. An American had visited a plant in Kiev which was using American machines to manufacture table cutlery. He pointed out to the engineer showing him around that one of the girls was misusing the stamping machine. Why not teach her how to do it? 'Not worth it. We have a labour turnover every week. That girl came in and said she had been driving a taxi and found the work unsuitable for women. So now she was giving the factory a go. Nobody thinks she'll stay.'

During our journey we met several men and women who, technically, must have been parasites, 'doing their own thing' and hoping the authorities would not notice. This is quite usual: the Soviet Union is far too big for the centre to keep tabs on everybody all the time. In some cases the anachronisms startle even the Russians. Vladimir Soloukhin, in his *Walk in Rural Russia*, was astounded to discover several villages not too far from Moscow where half the inhabitants had never joined any collective and, he said, still had the 'kulak' (independent farmer) mentality.

The low productivity of the Soviet workers astonished Western visitors. It takes at least two or three Russians to produce the average output of a Western worker. Part of the reason is inexperience: workers are often recent recruits from the countryside. In the town of Yevpatoria, a Pepsi executive found that no-one had even set eyes on a high-speed machine.

Moscow has one advantage in competing with the West: organised trade unions are instruments – not opponents – of the employer, in their case the state. President Brezhnev once told a trade-union conference that their job was to urge 'socialist emulation' (a euphemism for higher production) and to enforce labour discipline. He chided them for not doing as well as they should: 'Millions of man-days', he said, were being lost 'from absenteeism and idle time.' In relation to the management, Brezhnev promised the unions the Party's unqualified support for 'their just demands'. What is just is something for the Party to decide.

Driving through the Donets Valley we were at the heart of the coal-mining region. The mines are closed to foreign visitors but official reports on working conditions can be obtained from Intourist literature. Miners are paid the generous sum of between 300 and 350 roubles a month – more than twice the pay of a junior university lecturer. And they work a 30 hour week. But *do* they?

When I returned to Britain the TUC were quarrelling about whether to protest over the now celebrated case of the Donbas miner, Vladimir Klebanov, formerly a pithead supervisor. According to him, in order to fulfil the production targets, miners often have to work a shift of 12 hours, not 6, and they are sent down the mine with faulty safety equipment. He said that in the sixteen years he had worked there the mine had an average of between 12 and 15 deaths a year and 700 accidents. Having tried in vain to get conditions improved through the official channels, he had induced the workers to sign collective protests.

In Stalin's time, Klebanov would be languishing in some Arctic labour camp and credulous Western communists and 'fellow travellers' would be asserting that happy Soviet miners work only 30 hours a week. But these are not Stalin's days; and workers, particularly miners, can disrupt the whole economy.

For the last fifteen years a tug of war has been going on between the Party and its secret police, who want to keep Klebanov in gaol, and officials representing the legal and administrative apparatus, who want him freed. In 1964 the management dismissed him but, when they tried to evict the Klebanov family, these were protected by fellow miners. Bashkakov, Procurator of the Donets region, and I. Nikolayev, deputy head of the Ukrainian Department of Heavy Industry, upheld appeals against his dismissal. After he had been in and out of prison the courts in 1977 again found in his favour but the police took him off for 'psychiatric' treatment. In January 1978 he was released, and he concerted with other aggrieved workers and held a press conference. He and his friends were demanding not the right to strike (that would be unthinkable), but at least the enforcement by the managers of the existing safety rules and complaints procedures. Unlike most other industrialised countries, the Soviet Union refuses to publish any information at all about accidents at work.

In any country with independent trade unions, the ordeal of

Klebanov would be inconceivable – so much so, that many Western trade unions refuse to believe it. On the other hand, within the context of Soviet history, what is astonishing is that Klebanov was able to challenge the Party bosses and to give his cause international publicity.

This does not mean that all the mines we passed were as bad as Klebanov's. In some cases, there may indeed have been a 30-hour week and properly tested safety equipment. Tourists are not allowed to look and cannot know.

Even from our occasional glimpses, we could see that manpower shortage has made the workers harder to discipline. The fact that strikes are illegal does not mean they never take place. To prevent the risks of infection, the newspapers are not allowed to report such matters and the news filters through only slowly and indirectly. In his book *On Socialist Democracy* the Soviet writer Roy Medvedev complained that the Soviet news agencies frequently carry reports of Italian strikes, 'but nothing about the serious labour unrest in certain large cities and industrial centres at home. What were the workers' grievances and were their demands met? We do not know.' It seems that, since Stalin's day, Soviet management has lost the stick of terror without acquiring the carrot of economic incentives. And it is difficult to see how the economy can produce more of what the consumer wants while as much as *half* the total of Soviet machinery and equipment goes into armaments.

This astonishingly large proportion is not official; it is the calculation made by eminent Western economists using exclusively Soviet figures. They have taken the total value of the Soviet output of machinery and equipment and have subtracted every identifiable use to which it could be put within the civilian sector (investment, repairs and maintenance, output of consumer durables, everything which is publicly accounted for). They find they are left with 50 per cent of which the use remains unexplained and which, they presume, goes into military or paramilitary purposes.

In a narrow range of products, notably in aircraft, the military priority has a considerable civilian spin-off. Planes are plentiful and air fares cheaper in relation to earnings than in the West – though the accident rate is reputedly higher.

(Official figures are unavailable and unless there are foreign casualties accidents are rarely reported.) The Soviet aircraft industry has recently astonished the business world by breaking into the American domestic market. In the 1980s a Soviet Yak 40, a small but sturdy three-engined jet, designed to operate in tough climates and from short airstrips, will be flying in American skies. The Russians were eager for the deal but refused to allow the required on-site inspections of their production by the Federal Aeronautics Administration. So the Yak will be manufactured with Soviet equipment in the depressed steel town of Youngstown, Ohio.

It is always in the consumer sector that supplies fail to match demand. It would be dangerously misleading to forget that in some products the Soviet Union can stand comparison with any western country. But, while militarily useful industries flourish, the consumer has a lot to grumble about, and we heard a lot of grumbling. Take the case of Soviet cosmetics. Here the production is indeed rising but not nearly so fast as demand. Women are setting themselves new standards and any tourist who wants to make friends among the all-important *dezhournaya* at the hotels should arrive loaded with lipsticks and powder compacts.

A memorable case of a woman and daughter arrested for selling mascara manufactured from boot polish was reported in the London *Times* on 15 August 1978. They had set up a stall in an underpass in Moscow and soused the mixture in cheap scent in the hope of eliminating the smell. The offence is easily understandable, if you examine the figures provided by the Soviet Ministry of Trade for 1977: the Soviet cosmetic industry fulfilled only half the shops' order for lipsticks, one-third for mascara and just over a tenth for eye-shadow. The Soviet planners may feel they should give high priority to more laudable needs, but if they want to induce greater efforts among the new generation of women workers (the older ones managed perfectly well unpainted) they will have to waive their austerity and make greater allowance for feminine vanity.

Indeed, this would be to their own budgetary benefit: cosmetics are sold at a price far above the cost of production. There is now a lot of cash in circulation. If the cosmetics were available in the shops, the state would pocket big profits. Instead, the roubles go into the untaxed and untaxable black market.

From the political point of view, it can be argued that shortages help sustain the system. If you have the right connections, you can get almost anything. Some years ago, during the Khrushchev 'thaw' and before censorship was tightened up again, a Moscow comedian satirised a petty official: 'Comrades, shortages have made me who I am, shortages make me a person of substance and influence. So, comrades, what we want is shortages.' He need not have worried: shortages prevail everywhere in the Soviet Union – even in rich, disgruntled Georgia. This we discovered as we crossed the three consecutive road barriers separating the Russian from the Georgian 'Republic'.

14
Georgia: the One and Only

Georgia is one of the places that really does have to be seen to be believed. The land and its people are totally different from those in any other part of the Soviet Union – or indeed from any other part of the world. And the Georgian language, older than the Indo-European languages spoken in most of Europe, has no discernible link with any other.

Further, as the Georgians will not let anyone forget, their civilisation is older than the Russian. Christianity became the official religion of West Georgia about AD 330 and within the next two hundred years the whole of Georgia was converted. Placed along the caravan route from Europe to India, Georgia reached its apogee under Queen Tamara the Great, who reigned from 1184 to 1213. Then the population exceeded 100,000 and it was a flourishing centre of the arts, science, philosophy and religion.

It was not until the ninteenth century that Georgia was incorporated into the Russian Empire and, at the time of the Communist Revolution, the Georgians took Lenin at his word: he had promised to liberate the Tsar's subject peoples and, for three years, from 1918 to 1921, Georgia was an independent Republic, recognised by twenty-two nations, including Britain. Since 1921 it has again been ruled from Moscow though the Georgians are one point up: their capital, formerly known in Russia and internationally as Tiflis (see the

1914 *Baedeker*), is now officially and universally designated by its Georgian name of Tbilisi.

We arrived at Tbilisi, travelling east from the Black Sea, and left it, travelling due north, over the Caucasus. These drives were memorable both for the appalling quality of most of the roads and for the splendour of almost all the scenery.

Pelting rain damped our initial enthusiasm as we went through the picturesque first lap of the journey, taking us from Gagry to Ochemchiri, driving along between the Black Sea and the mountains. We zigzagged along precipitous slopes and caught only fleeting glimpses of our romantic surroundings through the windscreen wipers. Once it rained so hard that for a while we stopped altogether, wondering how on earth we would reach Tskhaltubo where we were to spend our first night in Georgia.

We had been told by Russians that in deserted Georgian roads it is common practice for the local police to hold up motorists and make them pay cash down, 50 or 100 roubles, for alleged infringements of the driving code. But they reassured us that foreign drivers are unlikely to be victimised if only because there is no common language in which business can be transacted. The Russians do not speak Georgian, but the Georgians do have a little Russian.

As we turned inwards to Tskhaltubo, a couple of young men coming the other way stopped their car and said the roads were so bad that we would never reach our destination that night. At that point a policeman arrived and said that although we still had several hundred kilometres to go, there was nothing to worry about, as we would be there before dark. Could he have been sober? If he had been right about the distance (in fact we had less than a hundred kilometres to go), he would have been wildly wrong about our chances of getting there. As we drove off, we heard him shouting to us to drive slowly.

Tskhaltubo is a small mountain resort, 280 kilometres from Tbilisi, and Intourist had warned us that they could not offer us *de luxe* accommodation. Still, it seemed odd that with so much rain and so many mountain streams the water in the local hotel was turned off between 10 p.m. and 7 a.m.

We had heard tales of the wildness of Georgian parties but

did not expect that on our first night the police would be called in to restore order. Margaret was in the bar when the brawl began. We discovered neither cause nor consequence, but Margaret saw a man, shirt covered in blood, staggering to his hotel room.

At Tskhaltubo we made friends with a Kurd from Tbilisi named Shamil, who lived up to the principle that man should laugh for fear of weeping. Shamil asked if he could join us for dinner and explained that he was a production engineer and had missed his train owing to the over-generous hospitality of the local man he was visiting, whose work he had been sent to inspect. Shamil felt he belonged to a permanently deprived minority – a nation without a home. He drew a diagram showing the Kurdish peoples scattered between several countries, none of which they can call their own. He saw the world as a huge joke against himself and the rest of humanity.

We offered to drive him to Tbilisi and he said he would think it over: the next morning he agreed to come. (We had precisely the opposite experience at Ordzhonikidze, north of the Caucasus: we met a majestic Ossetian girl who had been celebrating her medical graduation at a party in our hotel. She also said that she was going our way and the next morning would tell us if she could come with us. After our experience with Shamil we were sure she would. But the next morning she arrived with presents, hugged and kissed us goodbye, but politely declined the lift.)

Shamil's gaiety enabled us not only to survive but positively to enjoy our drive, over mountainous rocky tracks, of which about 44 kilometres were unpaved. He laughed at our groans and cheered us up with funny stories. As an Asian, he seemed to find the Russian dread of the Chinese particularly diverting, and this was the theme of his two best jokes.

The first was a television story. Before the main Soviet news bulletins, in the evenings, it is customary to give viewers a run-down of the weather and temperatures of the various parts of the USSR – complete with pictures of the local landscape. The shots of Moscow, the Arctic, Central Asia, the Pacific coast remind you – and are probably intended to remind you – that the Soviet Union is by far the biggest country in the world. The joke has a group of Soviet viewers sitting round their set unaware of a Chinese invasion and being startled to hear the weather man announce: '... and now, on the Sino–Finnish frontier ...'.

The second, rather longer joke involved Presidents Carter and Brezhnev. Brezhnev teasingly phones Carter and says: 'Mr President, I have had a very interesting dream'. 'What was it?' 'I dreamt that the White House was painted red and decorated with red placards.' A few days later President Carter rings Brezhnev and tells him that he has had an interesting dream. 'I dreamt that in Moscow the Kremlin was painted in red and decorated with red placards.' 'Yes,' says Brezhnev, 'but what did the placards say?' 'I'm sorry,' says President Carter, 'I don't read Chinese.'

The last part of the journey into Tbilisi was the most dramatic: we suddenly saw a series of caves, carved into vertical cliffs on the left of the road. They are said to have afforded refuge to the Christians at the time of the Mongol and Persian invasions. Then we descended into the valley of the Kura, which has hollowed itself a deep bed through the centre of Tbilisi. The water flows fast; the Kura river, in its south-eastern course through the town, has a fall of about 60 feet.

Tbilisi has prospered by being at the intersection of the trading routes from the Caspian to the Black Sea and also from the Armenian uplands across the Caucasus to Russia. Although Georgians predominate, the population is an astonishing racial hodge-podge, though Shamil was probably exaggerating when he said that there were a hundred different ethnic groups.

I had been given a preview of the wildness of life in Tbilisi six months before I arrived, when I met a bearded young Pole from Silesia at the Vnukhovo airport of Moscow. He had spent two years, and was planning a third, at the Tbilisi Engineering Institute. During a long talk, while our aircraft from Moscow to Warsaw was indefinitely (and inexplicably) detained, Stashek, as he was called, gave me a vivid account of 'the sheer anarchy' in Georgia. 'You can't imagine what it is like. No one obeys the law. They don't even pay any attention to the traffic lights.' On this last point he was certainly not exaggerating. Being driven through the centre of Tbilisi by a young

Georgian, son of a senior police officer and therefore able to travel without registration plates, was one of the most alarming experiences of my life. He not only ignored the lights. He also broke the speed limit, went the wrong way along one-way streets and ignored even the normal dictates of self-preservation.

Why should a Pole study in Georgia? Stashek explained that engineering graduates in the Eastern-European Comecon countries may pursue their studies in other parts of the communist bloc. The Moscow Institute had been his first choice, but it was full up. And as he had asked to be trained in the Soviet Union – an unusual choice for a Pole – he had been sent to Tbilisi instead.

The Polish authorities paid him a student grant of 250 roubles a month, which gave him a higher income than one of his Russian instructors who had been teaching in the Institute for ten years. What is the point of studying for years to qualify for the Institute? Stashek laughed: 'You know what the Russians are like. They all dream of belonging to the intelligentsia.'

Despite this example of non-materialist values, Stashek was astonished by the extent of corruption in Georgia – even though he himself was brought up in present-day Poland, where almost everybody either pays or receives bribes. In Tbilisi, Stashek had received 1,000 roubles (enough to buy himself a high-speed motor bike) from a Kurdish policeman in return for promising not to testify that he had been a passenger in a taxi when it killed a pedestrian. 'What a lot of money!' I exclaimed. The response was terse: 'It was nothing to what they had to pay the Procurator to keep the case out of court.' The Kurds are a tightly knit community and help one another. If the driver had been convicted, he would have lost his livelihood and probably been jailed.

Stashek also paid protection money. He was registered as an inmate of the international student hostel, whereas in fact he had shacked up with a Polish girl student in a private flat. He objected to being lodged in a corridor with Asians who, he said, were primitive and did not know how to use lavatories.

Corruption in Georgia is a matter of degree. It is less prevalent and barefaced under the present Party Secretary,

Ipokrat Shevardnadze, than it was under his predecessor, the now disgraced Vassily Mzhavanadze. In that period, whole industries flourished outside the law, acquiring their materials, machines and manpower by robbing state enterprises. Shevarnadze had also tightened up on black-market food. When I first visited Tbilisi in 1962, producers crammed their fruits, flowers and vegetables into the Soviet Aeroflot flights to Moscow (still remarkably cheap) and came home with tens of thousands of roubles in ready money. This is no longer possible; the scandal of the millionaire-gardeners had become too conspicuous.

The road barriers which marked our entry in and out of Georgia (in contrast to the absence of any sign when we crossed between the other Soviet Republics) were designed to prevent Georgian farmers off-loading their perishable commodities, especially meat, on the more lucrative Russian markets.

One result of these reforms is that the Georgians themselves eat a lot better than the other inhabitants of the Soviet Union. The luxury products of their farms – fresh meat, fruits and vegetables – now stay inside Georgia. When I was in Rostov, the shops had had no fresh meat or fish for almost a year. In Tbilisi both can be bought on the state-controlled counters of the regular retailers. As everywhere, the best quality is reserved for the private clientèle.

It was this 'anti-corruption' campaign which brought to a head the long-held grievances of the Abkhazians against the Georgians, of which I had first heard at Munich. The Abkhazian farmers evidently wanted to sell their products on the more lucrative Russian market and this seems to have inspired their proposal that they should secede from Georgia and incorporate their province into the Russian 'Soviet Federative Socialist Republic' (federative only in name). The component provinces of this giant territorial entity, which stretches all the way from Leningrad to the Pacific, have no autonomy and the RSFSR has none of the attributes of a federation. Moscow radio said the matter was being considered: as far as I know, it still is.

Only one aspect of Georgian life really shocked Stashek. 'Could you believe it,' he asked, 'they worship Stalin.' He said he had been brought up to believe that Hitler and Stalin were equally wicked, yet in Georgia Stalin was a national hero. There was even a portrait of the dead leader behind his Professor's desk. 'If you go to a banquet, you start by raising your glass to Stalin. Nobody even mentions Brezhnev.'

Is this really so? Bob Parsons, a Scottish graduate student who spent four months, from September to December 1978, in Tbilisi studying Georgian, recalled only two parties at which Stalin had been toasted. He was convinced that the Stalin cult survived only among the older generation; it had no devotees among his own educated and literary contemporaries.

Perhaps Parsons' contacts were more intellectual than Stashek's. When we stopped at Gori, Stalin's birthplace, on our way into Tbilisi, we saw pilgrims of all ages. They huddled together, buying Stalin badges, deferentially visiting his humble cottage now surrounded by massive marble pillars, and tramping over parquet floors through the huge halls, where pictures and mementoes were on display.

The photos included one of Stalin with Roosevelt and Churchill at Yalta and several family snaps, but none of his daughter Svetlana Alliluyeva, now in the United States. The museum was a very inadequate picture of Stalin's life and times: it left out the old Bolsheviks who helped him mould the country into its present form. Many of these have subsequently been rehabilitated (though not the two most important, Trotsky and Bukharin), but the curator of the museum could hardly have hung Stalin and his victims on the same wall. What counts in Georgian folk memory is that Stalin was a Georgian and ruled Russia. At a petrol station just outside Tbilisi, while Margaret was negotiating our petrol vouchers, a man got out of a small van and asked me where I came from and whether things were better in my country than in Georgia. Neither my Russian nor the circumstances were appropriate for a discussion about the advantages of living in a plural parliamentary democracy. So I simply said they were better in Britain: 'We have more meat.'

'Our stomachs are empty,' he said, pointing at his own. 'It was very different in Stalin's time. They looked after us then.'

'But wasn't Stalin a wicked man who killed many Georgians?' I asked mildly.

'That is what the Russians say. They want to discredit Stalin because he was a Georgian. You must not believe them. ...'

It is an amazing paradox that the Georgians still love Stalin yet are so patriotically Georgian, for, though Stalin (his real name was Josef Dzhughashvili) was born and educated in Gori, he more than anyone was the creator of the unitary Soviet state, which stamped out Georgian separatism and rejected any morsel of autonomy.

Though Georgia has its own culture, it is run politically like the other Republics, by the Politburo in Moscow, with the support of the ubiquitous secret police. Foreign visitors, however well disposed, are always suspect. One Western student, coming by train from Moscow, chatted with a passenger and asked for his address so that they could meet again in Tbilisi. But when he followed this up, he found that the 'address' was an uninhabited building site. Was the man an informer? Or just a Soviet citizen afraid of having foreign contacts?

Even a professor, Nia Abesadze, one of the least political people I ever met, was not above police suspicion. I had arrived with a letter of introduction to her from Dr Donald Rayfield, of Queen Mary College, London. Nia, who was a professor of Georgian literature, came to the hotel and presented me with souvenirs: a pretty enamelled brooch and an English translation of a well-known Georgian poet. We toured the city's churches and museums and met several of her students, who obviously loved her. Indeed, she had an infectious delight in the historical art treasures which the Georgians have lovingly preserved.

Far from being anti-Russian, she went every year to Moscow on holiday, going at least once a day – and sometimes twice – to the Russian theatre or ballet. Her two published books of lyrical poems qualified her as a member of the Soviet Union of Writers and in Moscow she stayed at the Writers' Club. She greatly admired Rayfield for his translations of Georgian literature and thought Tbilisi should erect a statue in his honour.

The current issue of one local literary review had published some of Rayfield's translations of contemporary Georgian verse and we went in search of a copy. We scanned the magazines in a kiosk on the main street and a Russian woman came out and started shouting at us: 'Hadn't we seen she was closing up? What were we doing? Did we expect her to work twenty-four hours a day?' I was taken aback but Nia laughed and told me not to worry. The different ethnic groups, she explained – Georgian, Russian, Armenian, Abkhasian, Ossetian, Kurdish, etc. – each specialised in their own occupations: the Russians monopolised the selling of newspapers. Nia said it was an old Russian custom to shout at people; she had not even noticed it.

During our walk, Nia showed me the impressively large public library and said it was much used by her students. Why did they not use the university library? It seems that in 1968 the authorities had agreed to build a new library. Since then, nothing has been built but during the waiting period all the books which arrived were left in their crates; if the students need volumes published later than 1968 they have to rely on the public library.

Several British scholars who have enjoyed working with Nia are inviting her to visit Britain. She is in her forties, certainly not sexually on the make, but has been refused an exit visa on the grounds that she is unmarried. 'Isn't it silly?' she said. 'If I'm not married yet it's hardly likely I would get married in England. Anyway I could not live anywhere but in my beloved Georgia.'

The Georgians are passionately attached to their own language and culture, in which they may find some compensation for their political subservience. When in 1978 the Party was reviewing the constitutions of all the Soviet Republics there were plans to eliminate the special clause which recognises Georgian as the official language. On 15 April, following a highly successful student 'demo', of which we were given a first-hand account, the plan was rescinded. Apparently without any previous organisation, more than 5,000 students poured into the streets. Soldiers were sent in to keep order, military vehicles cluttered the roads. Before nightfall, Party Secretary Shevardnadze came out of Party headquarters, walked across the central square and told the protesters not to worry: the language clause was safe. No disciplinary measures were taken against the students.

The victory was not good news for the 30–35 per cent of the Republic's inhabitants who are not Georgian and for whom, as a second language, Russian is more convenient than Georgian. Like old-fashioned colonists, the Russian minority (about 8 per cent) rarely trouble to learn the native language. When a Georgian-speaking traveller from West Germany went to buy his travel ticket at the Tbilisi Intourist Hotel, the Georgian girls at the counter teased one of their Russian colleagues: the German had been in Tbilisi for only four months and already spoke more Georgian than she did!

Georgians retain an unshakeable belief in their superiority over every other group – the Russians included. Racialism is endemic: ruthless economic and social discrimination is practised, particularly against the Asian minorities. The chief victims are the Kurds. Tbilisi is probably the richest city in the Soviet Union, but there were more beggars – mainly of Kurdish origin – than in any of the other cities we visited. Despite Moscow rule, Georgians do not feel the same animosity towards the Russians as, for example, the Irish towards the English. For Georgia has a far longer experience of being repressed by Mongols or Muslims than by Russians. By far the most destructive of the many invasions was by Genghis Khan in the thirteenth century. Fortunately, despite Hitler's exhortations, the German armies never managed to cross the Caucasus. The dread of Asia is still strong. The 'yellow peril' and the danger of an invasion by China is just as frightening to the Georgians as to the Russians.

Religion was one of the original bonds tying Georgia to Russia, and this may be the reason why Moscow has allowed greater freedom for the Church of Georgia than elsewhere in the Soviet Union. Thousands of people, young and old, attend the two big religious festivals at Mtskheta and Alaverdi, each lasting three days. They arrive in their own cars, in specially laid-on buses and trucks, or by horse transport. One foreign student had not troubled to ask permission when he went to the Mtskheta celebrations and there he ran into a member of the university staff. No need to worry: the man was hardly likely to draw attention to his own presence at the festival.

Religious themes still permeate contemporary Georgian art. In Tbilisi in the autumn of 1978, two theatre groups were simultaneously showing a tragedy based on the story of the woman martyr, Shushonik, who reputedly died rather than accept compulsory conversion to Muhammadanism. The Georgian Patriarch, Ilya (believed to be far less corrupt and less dominated by the KGB than his predecessor), went to the performance and was seen weeping.

A weird surrealist film on the theme of a religious festival, made a few years ago and still frequently shown, characterises the *avant-garde* and remarkably independent Georgian cinema industry. A sceptical hero watches, in a trance, as the strange religious rites unfold. A woman crawls on her hands and knees round the church. Finally he can stand no more, snatches a horse and gallops away. Recovering his senses he realises that the horse does not belong to him and returns to the village where the congregation gives chase. The film ends inconclusively with the now horseless hero gazing down from the church tower.

Georgians distinguish themselves from other Soviet peoples, not only in language and (apart from Catholic Lithuania) in the degree of religious observance, but also in their highly distinctive way of life. They are the Cavaliers to the Russian Roundheads. Vain, clothes-conscious, extravagant and exhibitionist, they also display a protective and chivalrous attitude towards women. Male travellers should be warned: Georgian women are beautiful but Georgian men are jealous. There was serious fighting in the university hostel in the summer of 1978 when Latin American students made what were thought to be improper advances to Georgian girls.

Unwittingly, even I caused a commotion. Margaret and I were visiting the steeply sloped botanical gardens with a group of young Georgians. We admired the view, took photos of us and them in mock embrace and we started back in time for a late dinner. Meals in Tbilisi are irregular. It was 10 p.m. before we sat down to eat a good Georgian feast, which we almost missed because of a stand-up row between our escorts.

Going down the hill one of the men, a little drunker than the rest, put his arm round my shoulder – mainly I think, to steady himself. We fell behind, chatting amiably, when the youngest of the men looked back and began hurling abuse at

him. He withdrew his arm and shouted back. It looked as if the
quarrel would end in blows – as quarrels in Georgia so often
do. As I could not understand a word of Georgian I asked the
girls, in Russian, what it was all about. They seemed
embarrassed and said it was a misunderstanding. Margaret
later discovered that the one who started the fuss was
objecting to his friend's behaviour and felt he was showing
excessive familiarity and lack of respect to a foreign lady.

The dinner party was in the famous restaurant on top of the
Mtatsminda (holy) Mountain. It was a noisy evening, with an
ear-splitting band, drink and dance, and we saw the ugly side
of the Georgian devil-may-care attitude. The centre of
attention was a boy of about nine years old with the face of a
cherub. He wore ragged clothes and had one sleeve coming
out of his jacket. He was evidently a familiar figure, well drilled
to elicit sympathy and charity. The whisper went around that
his father was in prison and his mother an invalid. When he
came to our table, one of our hosts took the child on his knee
and made him drink a glass of champagne at one go. The
child then danced alone, working himself into a frenzy with an
astonishing display of grace, rhythm and vitality. Later he
joined us again and boldly invited Margaret to dance with
him. When she went off with an adult, he sat back and lit a
cigarette.

The clients fondled and petted him and several gave him
cash. Later, when we were leaving, we saw him in the hall
counting his roubles. 'Look!' he exclaimed showing us eight
roubles – more than twice the average daily wage.

None of the Georgian men and women were in the least
perturbed. They regarded him affectionately, as if he were a
puppy.

Our next destination was Ordzhonikidze, just across the
Russian-Georgian border, and we travelled over the famous
military highway. According to *Baedeker*, the building of the
road took 53 years from 1811 to 1864; it proceeded at the same
time as the fighting. *Baedeker* describes the highway as 'one of
the most beautiful mountain roads in the world'. It was
certainly the most beautiful I had ever seen.

The peaks are always snow-covered, the rock is shiny black
or rich brown, the trees and grass, in many shades of green,

suggest the texture of soft velvet. We saw hardly any people except the occasional shepherd (one asked to buy cigarettes) but any number of animals. There were spotted pigs, mountaineering sheep, goats with corkscrew horns and thin cows clambering up slopes where, I thought, goats would fear to tread. Perched on the hills were numerous monasteries and villages, built by independent craftsmen and each different from the rest in shape and colour.

The aesthetic pleasure was enhanced by the element of physical risk. The road was twisting, the hills precipitous, the track narrow. In ravines below we saw several skeletal remains of vehicles. We went through long, black, unlit tunnels (childhood memories of ghost train terror) and had to cross fast-flowing mountain streams. Once, the road seemed to go straight over a waterfall. Margaret braked and asked, 'What do we do?' 'Put her in first gear,' I suggested, adding under my breath, 'and pray.' The car gurgled but never faltered. Then, even more suddenly, after a sharp turn, the road crossed another rapid. Margaret said later that the shock made the second incident even more alarming. But having discovered that our Volkswagen was amphibious, I no longer worried.

During most of our tour the ubiquitous Soviet lorries were a disagreeable impediment. But, on the military highways, we were only too pleased to follow in their trail. It was far easier to drive behind someone who knew the route, was familiar with the pitfalls and recognised which fork to take when – without signposts – the road suddenly divided.

When we neared the top of the Krestovski Pass, 2,459 metres above sea level, the slopes were covered in crisp snow. It was the middle of June but a snowfall the previous week had closed the highway for several days.

We stopped for a rest at a natural platform commanding a panoramic view and were joined by a group of construction workers on their way from Azerbaijan to Central Asia. We exchanged greetings (and more cigarettes) and they gave us four fresh lemons, our first since leaving Austria.

I asked the foreman why the streams on the highway were not bridged so that vehicles could ride over the rushing water. He said that the force of the water would knock down any construction. In any case, a safer road was now being built which would be open all the year round. When that happens they will presumably close the highway. I am glad we got there before it was too late.

I had visited Tbilisi once before by Aeroflot. But, seen from an aircraft, all mountain ranges look alike. If they have no car, tourists should settle for the railway and the bus. Indeed, many Russian holidaymakers cross the Caucasus by train, a journey which inspired a joke at the expense of Soviet farmers in the Russian satirical magazine *Krokodil*. A Russian traveller, surprised to see the mountains sooner than he expected, asks the guard whether they have already reached the Caucasus. 'No, these are the piles of unused fertilisers.'

And now a true story. A British diplomat who left Tbilisi by train heard the guard calling out, as they crossed the boundary of Georgia, 'And now we are entering the Soviet Union.' If a Soviet official had heard this private Georgian declaration of independence, there would have been trouble. Recklessness is a Georgian virtue.

15
Champagne on the KGB

Time was running out. We had given ourselves three weeks to reach Tbilisi but only one week for the journey home. Our Soviet visas expired on 3 July and we were to be in Budapest the next day where an old friend, the American Ambassador Philip Kayser, had invited us to the American Independence Party. It was the same landscape, scurried through more quickly, but the journey was memorable for four significant encounters.

The first was with a writer named Valery Kuz, a dapper young man whom we met at the Mashuk Hotel in Pyatigorsk, a health resort or, as the 1914 *Baedeker* has it, 'a watering town'. Its silt mud-baths are still widely patronised for medicinal purposes. Would we care to be interviewed? He wrote for the local newspaper and was sure his readers would be interested to read our impressions of Pyatigorsk.

Unfortunately we had no impressions of Pyatigorsk. After the dramatic drive from Tbilisi we had spent a lively evening at Ordzhonikidze. When we came down to dinner, we were joined by students celebrating their graduation, and invited to share their champagne. The next morning we left early for another tough day's drive to Pyatigorsk. After the usual tangle with one-way streets and ill-informed pedestrians, we managed to find our hotel, built palatially in 1902, and which we were told had once been patronised by the great Russian singer Chaliapin. He would certainly have felt at home in our splendid suite, with high ceilings, two balconies, spacious reception room and bedroom and roomy but old-fashioned bathroom. (The new functional furniture would certainly have shocked him). Instead of visiting the town, we had been glad to take a rest in our luxurious apartment.

Margaret had noticed Kuz standing outside the hotel when we arrived. Plainly he had been tipped off about our visit. He was well dressed, plump and affable, and Margaret, who likes identifying people with particular breeds of animals, said he reminded her of a pampered pekinese.

At dinner we saw him sitting with two women at a table near ours. It was clear that they were talking about us but Kuz did not approach us until we were leaving the restaurant. He did not seem put out by our inability to give him his interview. Later in the evening, however, he did say, a trifle reproachfully, that the article would have earned him 30 roubles (the equivalent, though he did not say so, of five litres of vodka).

As we had not yet had a chance to see Pyatigorsk, and as it was a clear moonlit evening, I asked him whether he would show us round. He did not have a car of his own (only, he assured us, because the newspaper provided him with a car and chauffeur whenever he wanted one). We had an enjoyable walk round this very green and charmingly situated little town. The name Pyatigorsk – five mountains – refers to the five peaks which surround it. Kuz pointed them out and told us their names. According to the legend, Mashuk, the name of one of the peaks and of our hotel, was a woman who died for love.

Though Kuz was diffident and respectful he wanted us to know that in Pyatigorsk he was a man of means and importance. His father ran an agricultural enterprise employing 10,000 men and he himself had travelled widely, visiting the Pacific, Siberia and Central Asia. He now looked forward to a visit to Britain, the prize he had won for a book about raising the level of cultural activities in rural Russia. He said that 52 million (out of a population of 261 million) Soviet people live on the land and that young people today wish to remain there but too often find themselves deprived of the cultural opportunities available in the cities. But if farming is modernised – as in the West – I asked, would so many people be needed on the land? Kuz said that the new generation, unlike the old one, loved country life. But what if this collided with the five-year plan? Kuz said people should be allowed to choose what they wanted to do.

The prize was a visit to any Western country. Kuz had chosen England because he dreamt of seeing the changing of the guard; also because he so much admired Winston Churchill.

Kuz said he would be coming to London the following February and we offered to show him the city. Unfortunately February came and went without a sign – a pity as, by that time, there were further matters I would have liked to take up with him.

Pyatigorsk, he said, was a city of great literary significance: Pushkin and Tolstoy were regular visitors and the poet and novelist Lermontov lived there during the last years of his life. Solzhenitsyn was born barely fifteen kilometres away. In view of what happened later, it is worth noting that it was Kuz and not I who raised this dangerously explosive name: several of the people we had met during our journey had mentioned Solzhenitsyn but always in a conspiratorial whisper.

Kuz begged us not to forget when criticising the Soviet Union that 'We are a young civilisation: only sixty years old.' But what about all those famous literary figures he had been talking about? Kuz made it plain that he was not one of those simple-minded Russians who indiscriminately worship the classics. Did we know that Lermontov used to write to his mama asking her to sell off a few serfs to pay his gambling debts? Kuz said his own research disproved the official story that Lermontov had been done away with by accomplices of the Tsar. The writer had died in a foolish duel, nothing to do with Nicholas I.

Kuz accepted that Leo Tolstoy was a great writer but he personally preferred Ivan Bunin (1870–1954), a White Russian who emigrated to Paris and whose best works are aesthetically erotic short stories. Bunin was the first of the very few Russians to win the Nobel literary prize. Bunin's work, like Stravinsky's, was banned in the Soviet Union until his death. Now, according to Sir Isaiah Berlin, Britain's leading scholar on

Russian literature, Bunin has become something of a cult in the Soviet literary world – though Berlin was surprised to hear that his fame had spread to Pyatigorsk.

After our walk, we asked Kuz to join us for a glass of tea in our sumptuous reception room. We discussed Soviet censorship and Kuz said he personally felt there should be a free exchange of newspapers and books. He admitted this was not official policy but he pointed out that the Soviet publishing-houses have printed many unorthodox writers who, he recalled, had in the past included Solzhenitsyn and Anatoli Kuznetsov. I pointed out that Kuznetsov's *Babi Yar* had been seriously expurgated (the Soviet censor had taken out everything critical of the Red Army or the Communist Party). But Kuz said that surely I, as a writer, had had my articles cut.

Kuz said he was writing an article on a hard-working tractor driver in the Pyatigorsk region who had ploughed within two years what had been planned to take five. (Margaret was reminded of a talented student she had met at Krasnodar who had failed to win a prize. 'It can't be helped' he told her, 'you see, I don't write about tractor drivers.' Kuz evidently did.)

We had another long day's drive ahead of us the next day and I told Kuz we needed an early night. He got up and kissed my hand. 'I must be a *gentleman*,' he said, using the English word, 'but I hope you won't mind if I ask Margaret to come with me so that I can give her some little souvenirs.' Margaret and he went up to his room, where he opened his case and brought out a selection of Russian short stories about animals with notes and a glossary in English. He asked her to wait while he wrote the dedication: 'In the hopes of meeting you again soon, be well and happy. Let there be peace. Valery, Pyatigorsk, June 1978'. Then, underneath, 'to my kind driver' – perhaps in anticipation of being driven round London. Kuz also gave Margaret a bottle of champagne for our journey. He could not have been nicer.

Our second personal encounter was in Poltava with Taras Nikitin, a poet. I use the epithet in the professional sense; I do not know whether he was poetically inspired, only that he earned his living by writing poetry as well as prose. He told us that if a journalist files a despatch in verse it is twice as well paid as it would be in prose. (Should the experiment be tried in the press of London or New York?)

On the way out we had had a shatteringly exhausting one-day drive from Kiev to Kharkov. On the way back we broke the journey at Poltava, famed as the site where Peter the Great defeated the Swedes.

Poltava was badly damaged during the last war and there was not much to visit. Our Intourist guide, Misha, a portly, jolly man wearing a bright red shirt and jeans, perspiring copiously, seemed quite as keen as we were to let us relax in peace. Misha said he had heard I was a journalist: would I like to meet a local writer? Indeed, I would. Poltava had no *de luxe* accommodation and our room was too cramped to receive visitors. We agreed that, after a couple of hours' rest, he would bring our visitor to the small lobby along the corridor which had imitation leather armchairs.

Whatever judgement one passes on the character of Taras Nikitin, he was certainly handsome. Also, in his salmon-pink shirt, knotted silk cravat and well cut trousers, he was ostentatiously smart. He told us that his mother had named him Taras after her hero, Taras Shevchenko, and always hoped he would be a poet.

Shevchenko (1814–61) the Ukraine's most famous poet, was bought out of serfdom by a group of Russian and Ukrainian intellectuals. He was banished because of his participation in a secret Pan-Slavic society, the Brotherhood of St Cyril and Methodius. Perhaps Shevchenko's dedication to the Brotherhood was an inspiration to his namesake's total dedication to the Communist Party!

Taras Nikitin had been brought up on a collective near Poltava, which is the centre of a region famous for its orchards. He told us that during his own lifetime (he was twenty-seven) he had seen the living conditions of the peasant improved beyond recognition.

We talked of education and he confirmed the information I had been given at Rostov that, under Khrushchev, the USSR had tried to raise the school-leaving age to seventeen. Since then, perhaps more sensibly than the British, Moscow has back-tracked. Now, non-academic children, from the age of fifteen, specialise in skills relating to their future jobs.

Taras said that on the collective farms specialist training starts earlier; by fourteen pupils begin to learn practical farming.

Fairly soon Taras steered the conversation away from Soviet domestic affairs. He told us he had recently travelled in Western Europe and had been very impressed by the strength of popular hostility to the neutron bomb. He was pleased to see that the opposition did not come only from workers. He had even met the daughter of a Dutch publisher who hung up an anti-bomb banner from her window. He seemed to think it particularly noteworthy that even the rich were responding. He asked what I thought of the Americans and, when I vaguely said I regarded them as allies, he protested that surely I could not support them after the war they had waged against the 'democratic forces' in Vietnam? But what is democracy? I asked. Neither the West nor the Communist Chinese regard modern Vietnam as democratic. This provoked Taras into retorting that, as we came from a country which was repressing the people in Northern Ireland and in which there were so many unemployed, we had no right to talk about democracy. From long experience, I am impervious to the Communist Party line. But Margaret, who normally switched off when the conversation became political or economic, suddenly blew up. She had no particular reason to feel patriotic. She was already nineteen when she came to England and still retains a Polish as well as a British passport, but she was not prepared to let a Soviet citizen lecture the British about democracy. The unemployed in Britain, she said, were better looked after than the fully employed in the Soviet Union and in Britain, though not in the Soviet Union, you have freedom of expression, meetings and newspapers. Taras and Margaret, roughly the same age, were going hammer and tongs when Misha turned up to say that, if we wanted to dine, the restaurant was now open. I invited Taras and Misha to be our guests at dinner so that we could continue the discussion. Taras and Margaret sank their differences when they discovered that they enjoyed the same pop groups and were both accomplished dancers.

While they were dancing I noticed two lonely-looking Americans and asked Misha to inquire whether, after their meal, they would join us for champagne. Mrs (Leslie) and Mr Murray Auerbach, from Hollywood, California, were old-time left-wingers, she more than he, and convinced the world was going 'the socialist way'. They were eager to see how the future worked. Obviously not rich, they had invested part of their savings in an Oldsmobile station wagon and were touring the camping-sites in the Soviet Union. I found their innocence touching. They were probably too old to take on board the revelations about the Gulag and they arrived full of hope and good will.

Having travelled widely in the United States and knowing California well, I recognised this state of mind. The trouble was that the Soviet officials did not. When the Auerbachs arrived at the frontier, they and their car were submitted to a search which lasted six hours. The Russians were trying in vain to discover what these curious Americans were up to. By the time the Oldsmobile, which had been wholly dismantled, had been put back together again and they were allowed through, it was almost dark. They were being looked after by a tough blonde woman who, from their description, must have been the one in charge of us when we reached the frontier three days late.

She told them they must press on to Lvov, on the other side of the mountains. We had spent our first night at Uzhgorod, which has in Intourist hotel but not an Intourist camp-site. Even travelling fresh and by daylight, the journey over the Carpathians had been harrowing. The Auerbachs had been compelled to drive through the night and confessed they had been 'absolutely terrified'. But they were not down-hearted; they would press on.

The Americans had seen Taras and Margaret go off together and said it looked like love at first sight. Later, when they returned, we drank toasts, the Auerbachs excused themselves and I called for the bill. 'No, no,' said Taras, 'the evening is on me.' In retrospect, I believe the KGB must have paid. Never mind, it was a relief not to have to change another £35 to pay for the four meals and two bottles of champagne.

Before leaving, Taras gave Margaret a book of poems by young Poltavans, which started with verses of his own. Each set of poems was preceded by a photo and potted biography of the writer. From these we learned that Taras used to wear a moustache, that he was a Party Member, had once worked on the railways and had graduated from the Poltava Pedagogical Institute.

He dedicated his book to Margaret in terms that were noticeably less effusive than Kuz's: 'To Margaret Moss: May the verses about Poltava be read also in faraway England.' In order to have them read in 'faraway England,' we needed to find someone who could read Ukrainian. Victor Swoboda, senior lecturer in Russian and Ukrainian at the School of Slavonic and East European Studies, generously read them on our behalf. The poems, Swoboda said, were gushingly patriotic but the patriotism was Soviet and not Ukrainian. One poem entitled 'Quest' claimed that the Soviet motherland 'blesses us tenderly' for Soviet scientific, industrial and agricultural achievements. The poem ends: 'Orders and medals, like landmarks on the conquered summit of our dreams' – a thought appropriate to a young man who, according to his biography, had already won two literary prizes.

One poem is addressed to a ghost commissar leading the ghost soldiers of his regiment, who rise from under the obelisk and hurl themselves into the attack. Another is in praise of a mother heroine (in Soviet parlance a woman decorated for having ten or more children). A third is 'a ballad about the richest woman', addressed to Kateryna Padusenko, a worker in a forestry team who feels that the forest is hers.

Swoboda gives his own rendering of one verse of a poem entitled 'Return': 'Is there anything / More beautiful on Earth / When combine harvesters / Like red cranes / Fly over the steppe / Into the glimmering distance. ...' My answer would be an unqualified yes, there is! But Taras was plainly not a preservationist.

Could Taras have written all this with his tongue in his cheek? He double-crossed us and may have double-crossed the Soviet censor. The poems of the thirteen other young Poltavans are generally more lyrical and less obviously contrived in order to please the Party.

Getting published in the Soviet Union is not easy, as I discovered from another Soviet poet I met during our journey.

A first book has to be accepted by the publishing house in the district where it is written; if the Party man in charge dislikes it, there is no appeal. A second work, however, even if rejected in the home town, can be submitted elsewhere. All the editors are under Party control but they might have different tastes. My informant had been told that his poems were interesting but could not be published without an ideological commitment. He dug out a poem he had written in praise of Lenin for his school magazine. He submitted it with some embarrassment but it served its purpose. This childhood poem was placed first in the book and the poet is now an accepted Member of the Soviet Union of Writers.

Taras's poem may have been a cover for the more serious writings of his colleagues who – like Margaret's Krasnodar friend – could not bring themselves 'to write about tractor drivers'.

The third and most interesting of our encounters, and the only one we initiated ourselves, was with the Professor of Journalism at Kiev University, Vitaly Gregorovich Toichkin. One of Toichkin's former students, whom we got to know in Rostov, thought he might be going to Kiev and could meet us again on our way home. He did not know where he would be staying but said we could reach him through the Toichkins, whose telephone number he gave us. Our friend never turned up but we thought it would be interesting to meet the Professor. We rang up and he invited us to his flat at 6.30 that evening. It was an easy trolley-bus ride from the hotel. We found him alone, wearing a denim shirt and jeans, watching an international football match. He received us amiably; we begged him not to let us disturb the game but he switched it off and invited us to join him in a drink of an excellent liqueur, a regional speciality.

We chatted about our trip and the people we had met. I commented on the ethnic jumble and expressed surprise that so many students appeared to be studying so far from where they were born. Toichkin said this was part of a deliberate policy of integrating the various ethnic groups. The traditionally rival peoples would merge ultimately into the Soviet citizen – he used the Russian words though *civis sovieticus* might have been equally appropriate. The loyalty and patriotism of this new species would be directed to the whole Soviet community.

Another point we commented on was the keenness we observed about motor cars and consumer goods. In Kiev at the time we were there, a pair of high-quality Western jeans (of the kind the professor was wearing) were fetching 200 roubles – more than a month's average wage. Like many Western university teachers, Toichkin deplored the frivolity and idleness of the young: they failed to appreciate the sacrifices their elders had made to enable them to live an easy life (I was reminded of a British academic who refers to his students as 'welfare puddings'). Vitaly's anxieties were very much like those expressed to me by the industrial editor of *Pravda*, upon whom I had called when visiting Moscow earlier in the year. He said that if I wanted to appreciate the pioneering and creative spirit of the young Communists I should go to Siberia. Apparently Kiev as well as Moscow had been corrupted by the life-style and permissive habits from the West.

Suddenly the front door opened and the flat filled up. In came Mrs Toichkin, an Airedale dog, a son and daughter (aged ten and eight): good old-fashioned children, seen and not heard, and Vitaly's mother-in-law. They had come back by car from their country dacha. We had already seen the flat's other inmates: two magnificent Siamese cats and a cage of budgerigars. After introductions and greetings the children and the dog withdrew and the adults and the cats settled down for a quiet evening.

We discussed Toichkin's work and he said that in Kiev, as in most Soviet universities, journalism is a branch of the philology department. Was Toichkin's work made difficult by the Soviet ban on foreign newspapers? He said he read what he pleased and proved the point by bringing in an armful of copies of the French newspaper *Le Monde*. He flatly denied a fact known to every foreign visitor to the USSR: no western journals except Communist ones are publicly on sale in Soviet shops or newspaper stands.

How could aspiring journalists understand contemporary Soviet history, I asked, when there was still a blanket of secrecy about the Stalinist period and as long as the famous Khrushchev report, recounting Stalin's crimes, was suppressed? Toichkin denied any such thing. All the universities, he said, had copies of the proceedings of Party Congresses and in these students could read what Khrushchev had said. It was not until I got back to London that I was able to consult the published verbatim reports of the Twentieth Congress. Khrushchev spoke twice: the first time he gave a long account of Government policy, which is published in full. The second time the printed text merely says, in ten lines, that in secret session he discussed the errors of the 'cult of personality'.

Toichkin told us he himself lectured on the 'mistakes' of Stalin's agricultural policy. He must have known that the collectivisation had been particularly agonising in the Ukraine. Anatoli Kuznetsov's father had been a Party member and had told his son how the peasant families had been starved into submission and reduced to cannibalism. He recounted how a peasant family was once found making a meal of the body of one of their children. The officials decided not to make a criminal charge; they took the lot into the woods, shot them and buried the bodies. The deportations and murders of millions of farmers were manifestly outside the university curriculum.

Mrs Toichkin served coffee, freshly baked biscuits and soft-centred sweets. She said she was a journalist and wrote on local Ukrainian affairs. Her mother, a professor of literature, told us that although she was above the retiring age both staff and students had entreated her to stay: Kiev was seriously short of university teachers. When Margaret lamented that, even with an honours degree from London University, she could not get a job suited to her qualifications, Toichkin's mother-in-law said she should come and work in Kiev.

Did he know why Soviet officials were so eager to separate foreign visitors from the Soviet public? Many of the people we met were afraid to come into the Intourist hotel. The Toichkins said it was only for our own protection; criminals had burned down a hotel in the middle of Moscow. It was better to restrict admission than to risk violence.

Our hostess and her mother then turned the tables on us.

When they visited England they found people much less friendly than the French. And how could we speak of intellectual freedom when a Soviet professor was not allowed to deliver a lecture in Oxford until he had cleared his text with the university authorities? As an Oxford graduate, I protested this could not be so: there is no Oxford body empowered to dictate to the separate colleges. Mother-in-law was firm: 'I happen to know it is true.'

Toichkin deplored the damage President Carter's human rights policy was doing to détente. He saw the campaign as a deliberate ploy to worsen relations and claimed that the rights of a Soviet citizen were much better protected than the rights of a Harlem black. His only visit to the West had been to Quebec. Had he met any of the large colony of Ukrainians in Canada? Certainly not! They were traitors who had fled during the war.

He ignored the fact that most of the Ukrainian colony in Canada arrived in the early part of the century not from the Russian but also from the Austro-Hungarian Empire and from Poland. The ones who got out during the last war were the lucky ones: most Ukrainians who were sent back died in labour camps.

Continuing their counter-attack, the Toichkins said that, whereas their bookshops were full of translations of contemporary British and American works, no Soviet literature was ever on sale in the West. There is in fact an unprecedented boom in modern Russian literature – both in hard back and paperback. But I did not mention it as all the popular authors are dissidents.

Despite our differences, we left on friendly terms. The mother-in-law suggested that we should stay for supper but we thought it improper to intrude any longer. As we were leaving we exchanged hopes that we would meet again. It was only after my return to London that I found out that Professor Toichkin had once been in the Party's black books, and that the secret police, with their elephantine memories, were probably still watching him. I stumbled across his unusual name in a report on Ukrainian nationalism by Roman Solchanyk, published by Radio Liberty's research department. Sovietologists in London confirmed that Toichkin's name figures in a group of journalists who had protested in 1964 against the punishment of Matvii Shestopol, an assistant professor of journalism who had publicly advocated the wider use of the Ukrainian language. Shestopol had protested against the current Communist practice of treating the advocacy of Ukrainian as evidence of 'bourgeois nationalism'. He was dismissed and expelled from the Party. According to a samizdat document dated 1966, Shestopol's supporters, including Toichkin, were dismissed from their jobs or incurred other Party and Komsomol penalties. The document does not say what these penalties were. For eighteen months Toichkin apparently published nothing. Since then it seems he has been a member of the journalistic faculty of Kiev.

Shestopol has now recanted. In February 1978 he published an article conceding that 'In the past, certain representatives of the cultural front (presumably including himself and Toichkin) were the subjects of just criticism'. What I heard in the Toichkin drawing-room was a replica of Shestopol's article in which he similarly lambasted the American 'ideological offensive'.

Looking back, I am amazed that Toichkin invited us to his home. He and his womenfolk were well advised not to deviate one iota from the Party line. If the house was bugged the police knew what they said. If not, this book recounts the conversation. Either way, the Toichkins said nothing to which the Party could object. Nor do I blame the family for taking precautionary measures, after we had left. They were now part of a privileged élite and had a lot to lose.

The last and least rewarding of our encounters took place in the Intourist restaurant at Lvov against the deafening din of a pop band. A man who never told us his name came and sat next to me. He was stocky and ugly; he had a red nose and over his vodka and herring complained bitterly that the services in the hotel were not what they used to be. I asked him whether he was from Lvov and he said that his father was an army officer so that they had no fixed home. He was now a chemical engineer, and had decided to settle in Lvov. He told me he was Jewish, which seemed odd, because Jews were rarely, if ever, professional army officers. I asked if there was any anti-Semitism in Lvov: 'Yes,' he said, 'it is terrible!'

I said I had been astonished to hear that Jews had their racial identity marked on their passports. Could I look at his, to see how Jewishness is registered? He snapped back that he did not have his passport with him.

The food was poor, the noise was dreadful, the company boorish. We got up to leave and he followed us and suggested another drink. We refused. We wanted to make an early start the next morning to enjoy what was supposed to be the last day of our Soviet tour.

16
Mutt and Jeff

We left Lvov in bright and warm weather and this time really enjoyed our journey over the Carpathians. The unpaved dirt-tracks, which had so alarmed us on the way in, were now a familiar experience and Margaret had learnt how to circumvent trucks and tractors. Coming in, our eyes had been glued to the road. Now we could relax, knowing the Volkswagen could take it, and stop where we pleased for a rest or a bite (this time we had sensibly stocked up in advance). We were able to admire the steep, jagged hills with trees growing right to the mountain tops and the narrow uncultivated valleys full of wild flowers and we were never far from the sound of cascading water. It had been a wet season. Now, in the sunshine, everything sparkled.

There was just one worry: where would we spend the night? I intended to cross into Hungary and count on my hard currency and Hungarian good will, to find a room in an inn or private home. During the summer months all Budapest hotels are jammed and our booking for the Hilton was only for the next day, 4 July. As it turned out, my anxiety was misplaced.

At 6 p.m. we reached the frontier, where we were greeted by the steely-eyed, well-groomed blonde who had been so unkind to our friends, the Auerbachs. At first everything went well. The officials approved the chit on currency transactions which has to be handed in before leaving. Intourist paid us back for our unused petrol voucher in hard currency (dollars: they apologised for having no sterling) and nobody objected when we declined a request to inscribe an appreciative comment in the Intourist's visitors' book.

Then the customs check. I said I hoped it would not take long. The Intourist woman said the average was about fifteen minutes. We left 24½ hours later.

A boorish official, assigned to handle our personal possessions, had very little to inspect. We had not brought in many clothes (there was never any need to dress up) and in the Soviet Union had purchased only one garment, an embroidered shirt made for a man but which Margaret fancied for herself. We had accumulated a large bulk of Soviet literature – books, pamphlets, periodicals, newspapers, guides, maps, menus, etc. – but these were taken away for special scrutiny. Our sparse private belongings, mostly underwear and toiletry, were spread over several metres of the customs counter and every item was fingered and poked. The inspector opened and squeezed the toothpaste tube. He saw something sinister in a pair of my sandals, in which the inside-sole of one shoe, but not the other, was loose. He sent both down for expert analysis. He found a piece of cleaning-leather stuck at the bottom of my spectacle case and when I failed to extract it he snatched the case away to see for himself.

He peered into the pipe I had bought as a present for my husband. The bowl was carved into the shape of Lenin's head; an appropriate receptacle for conspiratorial messages.

At first it was hard not to laugh but, after an hour of standing watching this performance, I got tired and said I hoped he would not mind if I sat down. Sit down I did, but he sniffingly indicated that he found my nervousness suspicious.

Once again, a team of mechanics took the Volkswagen apart and examined all the bits. Fortunately there were not as many as in the Auerbachs' Oldsmobile. We were then taken to the basement, where an obviously embarrassed woman soldier searched our bodies. Recognising that I was ticklish, she did not touch the more sensitive parts of my anatomy. After that, into the main lounge expecting to retrieve our documents and leave. Then a soldier asked me to follow him. We went back to the basement where three men were sitting at one end of a table and I was directed to a chair opposite.

'We have questions to ask you,' said the top man, a stocky, saturnine figure who looked like a caricature of a KGB interrogator – but turned out to be a real one. 'We have reason to believe that you came here, not as you claim for touristic reasons, but to engage in activities harmful to the Soviet Union. We have evidence that you have violated Article 62 of the Criminal Code of the Ukrainian Soviet Socialist Republic by carrying on "anti-Soviet agitation and propaganda" – for which the penalty is the maximum of seven years' imprisonment.'

'This is absurd!' I said. 'But if you are preferring legal charges against me I must insist immediately on being put in touch with our Consulate in Moscow and with my lawyer, Lord Goodman, who has considerable experience in dealing with Soviet authorities. Also I would like to send a message to Her Majesty's Foreign Secretary, Dr David Owen, who is a personal friend.'

The KGB man said: 'It is for *us* and not for you to decide when you may communicate with the outside world.' I did not argue, though I knew that under international law the decision was mine and not theirs.

Then I was asked many times over why I was in the Soviet Union. Answer: to see places and to meet people. Who had paid? I had – having told the Soviet Embassy in advance that I proposed to recoup the cost by writing articles about my tour. For whom was I working? For myself.

We had a long argument, in which a second interrogator participated, about the nature of propaganda and how it can be distinguished from ordinary conversation. A third man, tall, doleful and friendly, acted as interpreter. I understand Russian but preferred to answer in English. I corrected him when he failed to get my point. He got into trouble telling the interrogator that I could not understand the difference between propaganda – which was forbidden – and trying to convince people in private talk, which was presumably allowed. 'She understands very well!' roared his boss. 'She just pretends she doesn't.'

Was I familiar with the final act of the Helsinki Agreement? Yes. Was I aware that my government was a signatory to this important international document? Yes, again. Then why had I violated Clause 6, which commits the signatories – and here he began reading the text – 'to refrain from any intervention, direct or indirect, individual or collective, in the internal or external affairs, falling within its domestic jurisdiction ...'. On the contrary, I replied, my journey was perfectly within the spirit of Helsinki. The British Government would never have signed an agreement curtailing the freedom of speech.

The Russians, I was told, had read my articles on Comecon in the magazines *Foreign Policy* and *The Banker*, which had been seized on my way in (with a token promise that they would be returned when I left). These showed I was 'unfriendly' to the Soviet Union. Yet the articles had earned the approval of Sam Pisar, the international lawyer who has been the foremost American champion of détente and East–West trade.

The interrogation (or, sometimes, argument) lasted nearly three hours. When I got home, friends asked whether I had been scared. Not in the least. My first reaction had been astonishment. Then that unique journalist's thrill when a good story falls into one's lap. It was not because I was innocent that I knew I had nothing to be afraid of. If the secret police had been out to get me, innocence would have been irrelevant. But I was certain the Soviet Government could not want the international commotion which would have been provoked by my arbitrary arrest. Not that I counted for much myself. But, having spent my life as an international reporter, it was my business to know anybody who was anybody. My ten years in the parliamentary lobby, as *The Observer's* political correspondent, meant that I knew all Britain's leading politicians. I had also got to know most of the Common Market Commissioners in Brussels, President Giscard d'Estaing in Paris and Henry Kissinger and Zbigniew Brzezinski in Washington. I had been Paris correspondent at the same time as Ben Bradlee, now editor of the *Washington Post*, and Moscow correspondent with Max Frankel, now editor of the *New York Times*. I was asked, in a threatening way, if I knew that there were criminal charges against two American journalists. The correspondents of the *New York Times* and the *Baltimore Sun* were at the time being accused of slandering Soviet television. Predictably, neither of them came to grief any more than I did.

Finally, I was told I must spend the night in Chop. The chief interrogator said menacingly that he hoped I would be more co-operative after I had had time to think things over. The second interrogator said he regretted that the available accommodation was not top-class. I told him not to fret.

Margaret was not aware of the extent of my international network and therefore easier to intimidate. I had no chance to reassure her as they took her down one stairway while they were taking me up another one. For several hours they grilled her about her relationship with me and she had the feeling they were trying to get her to frame me. Had she not been an innocent decoy, whom I was exploiting for my anti-Soviet purposes? Upstairs, a policewoman, flanked (and now and again assisted) by our Intourist blonde, was sitting at a large round table sorting out and translating into Russian the handwritten material found in our luggage. I had made fairly prolific notes but they were no use to them as my handwriting is illegible – even to me. Margaret's diary, on the other hand, was a neatly written log-book of the times we arrived, what we ate, and where we stayed. She had written it in English and it was being translated word for word into Russian.

It seemed silly to sit doing nothing and I conveniently remembered a delightful book Margaret had been given at Krasnodar and which I had intended to borrow. It was an illustrated collection of 594 Russian idioms with English translations. I told them the little black volume must be among the stuff on the table and it was found and handed back to me.

Time flew as I made my way through the pages, writing down the idioms which I wanted to learn. Two seemed particularly appropriate to our present situation. One was 'to make an elephant out of a fly', which is the Russian for making a mountain out of a molehill. The other was 'to meet someone with bayonets', the Russian way of describing a hostile reception: the cartoon showed Copernicus getting into trouble for saying that the world was round. When I came to these two I showed them to our Intourist guide. She returned them with an icy smile.

The motor car was the theme of many of the illustrations, even though the idioms dated from long before the discovery of the internal combustion engine. The Russian 'to kill two hares' – in English, killing two birds with one stone, featured a cheerful man playing a concertina and pumping the air into a flat tyre. 'The golden mean' – identical in both languages – had a policeman watching three cars: one dragging behind, one speeding ahead and a sensible one chugging along with the speedometer indicating medium. 'To be born under a lucky star' was illustrated by three cars in an unholy crash and a man in the middle lucky to be alive.

There was even an idiom for the Beatles. The Russians words 'from someone's light hand' were interpreted to mean: 'initiatives following someone's example, which set in motion a series of subsequent actions or deeds'. The pictures showed the four Beatles strumming their guitars and eight more little men strutting along wearing the Beatle hairdo. I found two idioms to boost Margaret's morale: 'To be not of the timid dozen' – meaning 'not easily frightened' or 'not cowards'. And, to cheer her animal-loving heart, 'To heave a sigh of relief', illustrated by a picture of a grinning deer crossing the line marked 'nature reserve', just as the hunter intended to shoot it.

My favourite cartoon in the book was somewhat surrealist: 'the latest cry of fashion' – a picture of two women wearing fox furs round their necks and upstaged by a woman wearing a large fish.

Later, in the general confusion when our stuff was being piled back into the car that was to take us to Chop, a bundle of translations was mistakenly included. They were not very accurate. On one occasion, at Sochi, we had noticed a British car parked outside the hotel and left a letter on the windscreen addressed 'Dear driver', saying that if he was a compatriot he might like to join us in the restaurant for a drink. The man was an Australian and when he came he brought in my letter, which I forgot to throw away. I hope he will not be offended to know that, in translation, I address him as 'chauffeur'.

The ladies had also translated a note from the two English teachers at Rostov warning that communications might be difficult as, in taking messages, their woman caretaker was 'not very helpful'. In Russian, the translation came out as 'unable to help'. Could it have been a deliberate mistake, a show of solidarity between petty bureaucrats?

Before they let Margaret go, they warned her not to try to

communicate with the outside world. There was no telephone anyway.

We were told to take our things and the woman policeman drove with us in our car to Chop. I told a soldier that I was too tired to pick up my bag and waited while he hesitated and then carried it for me to the car. Evidently I was still a tourist, not a prisoner.

It is unusual for foreign visitors to be admitted to non-Intourist hotels. Though we had a bathroom and lavatory, the water was turned off. The night receptionist said it was impossible to make tea. The hotel was next to the railway station and the walls were so paper-thin that the announcements of arrivals and departures sounded as if they were being made inside our bedroom. Chop is a busy junction and trains were coming several times an hour. The monotonous voice of the female announcer lulled me to sleep. Margaret was too nervous either to sleep or eat. I woke up with a huge appetite and found a station bar where I had tea, omelette, bread and butter. It was the only meal of the day.

We had been told to return at 8 a.m. For two hours we were totally ignored. They took Margaret first. But this time I had reassured her and from her account it seems she gave as good as she got. Now a new interrogator had come in, an elegant fair-haired man who said the same kind of things in a much nicer way. I guessed he came from Moscow and was junior in the administrative hierarchy, but senior in the power structure. At the time, I thought the contrast between the two men was accidental. Later I learnt that it is standard practice in police interrogations. In his book *America in Vietnam*, Guenter Lewy writes of a technique known as 'Mutt and Jeff', which, he says, was authorised by the US Army field manual on intelligence: 'This ruse involves the use of two interrogators, one of whom is tough and aggressive while the other is friendly and sympathetic.' We did not know about Mutt and Jeff and called ours Toughy and Smoothy.

Toughy told Margaret that he hoped she would come clean as he had beside him a bundle of letters from Soviet citizens proving our guilt. He then proceeded to name those who, he said, had signed letters protesting against our anti-Soviet activities. From what we later put together there were four:

Valery Kuz, of Pyatigorsk, alleged we had said that the Soviet Union was not a democracy. Taras Nikitin, of Poltava, recorded that we had criticised Soviet military policy. Mrs Toichkin (the wife of the Kiev professor) complained that we had come to their flat uninvited and had spoken adversely of the USSR. And the unnamed man from Lvov claimed that I had told him that Jews should emigrate as they would be better off outside the Soviet Union.

How could Margaret account for these complaints? She said that the people must have misunderstood what we were saying. She was asked whether she did not feel she was abusing Soviet hospitality (at £21 a night hospitality was hardly the appropriate term) but she retorted that she had had a most agreeable visit. 'Then why do you say in your diary that at one hotel the sheets were dirty?' 'Dirty and torn' Margaret corrected. But how would she feel if she had a guest in her home who said that the chair was crooked and the glasses were dirty? 'I would give him a straight chair and wash the glasses.'

The dreaded name of Solzhenitsyn came into Margaret's interrogation but not into mine. We were accused of propagating his works. In fact it was our Soviet hosts and not we who had so often brought his name into the conversations.

Toughy said to Margaret that he expected we had seen Soviet army vehicles as we approached the frontier (we had indeed observed a huge fleet of them) and presumably would go home and say that the Soviet Union was preparing an attack on the West? No, said Margaret, recalling our conversation as we passed them, we thought the Soviet Union must be holding military manoeuvres. 'Quite wrong,' said Toughy. 'The soldiers were being brought in to help with the harvest!'

Some of the questions put to Margaret were highly personal. Why had she gone to England? Why was she not with her husband? What were her politics? Did she vote in British elections? This was rich from people who were lecturing me about non-interference in the domestic affairs of another country. Margaret had been brought up in Poland and had no particular feelings about secret ballots. She answered that all her husband's family voted Labour and so did she.

She was told she must make a written report on her whole journey.

'In Russian or in English?'

'As you like.'

'I will do it in Russian.'

'Excellent, it will be good practice for you.'

It took Margaret three hours to compile the day-by-day report. Smoothy came several times to volunteer advice. He insisted that the document must contain an apology. 'But I haven't done anything wrong!' 'You must ask the Soviet Government to forgive you.' Smoothy also asked whether she knew that I had been associating with 'criminal elements'. Margaret asked if he meant Anatoli Kuznetsov (whom she had met in my home in London). He said yes. Margaret asked if they would have minded if we had taken a letter to Kuznetsov's old and ailing mother. 'Of course not, we've nothing against her. It is her son who betrayed us.'

Then, my second interrogation. It took almost four hours, but this included long interruptions while Smoothy and Toughy went off to confer with each other or with Moscow. During these intervals the interpreter stayed with me, and his conversation indicated that he did not consider me a criminal. He asked what I thought of Scotland's defeat in the World Cup. It was the first I had heard of it but I concealed my ignorance and said it was very sad.

Certain material in my possession should not be taken out of the Soviet Union, I was told. What material? Two education manuals which I had been given at one of the universities and two local newspapers, one from Zaporozhye and the other from Krasnodar. Later, while I was alone with the interpreter, I asked him why it was that only national newspapers printed in Moscow could be taken out of the country. He said it was because local journals often attack the administration, and critical material would be seized upon by the Western press.

The interpreter tried a softer approach. 'Surely you would agree', he said, 'that there is no racial discrimination here, as there is in Britain.' (Soviet television had been featuring racial incidents in British towns.) No, I would not agree. I did not take up the question of the Tartars, Jews, and other racial minorities who are certainly discriminated against, but I told him of an incident recounted by English visitors to Rostov who had invited a Kenyan student to the 'hard currency' bar at the main hotel. The Russian barman told them they could order what they liked but he would not serve the black man; the blacks 'could climb back into the trees'. The interpreter said that was 'just an unfortunate exception'. I said we had unfortunate exceptions too.

Whereas all four informers were mentioned to Margaret, I was told of only two – our Poltavan poet and the *agent provocateur* at Lvov. Toughy complained that I had talked to a young, unbriefed journalist about sensitive issues of national defence. If I wished to discuss such matters, meetings should be arranged through appropriate channels. I pointed out that it was Taras and not I who had diverted the conversation from domestic to international affairs. No one would come to the Soviet Union to inquire about the neutron bomb. As for the man from Lvov, he was lying: I had never mentioned the subject of Jewish emigration. 'Why should we take your word against the word of a Soviet citizen?' asked Smoothy.

I, too, was told that I must draw up a statement on the tour and answer the allegations against me. Foolscap sheets of paper were provided and I was left alone with the interpreter. I wrote in enormous characters that I had come as a tourist and talked to people about any questions which had interested them. Smoothy looked at my copy and complimented me on my style. I reminded him that writing was my profession.

He insisted that the script should be addressed to the Soviet Government. We then began arguing about an additional paragraph in which he wanted me to apologise. We reached a compromise: I have no copy of the script but, as I recall it, I said, 'I regret that the officials felt the need to cross-question me about my meetings with Soviet citizens.' Perhaps I should have been adamant against using the word 'regret'.

Strictly speaking I did not regret anything, least of all the interrogation itself, which was an interesting experience. But I was in a hurry to leave. I was still counting on reaching Budapest in time for the American Independence party. Nor did I feel that the text, manifestly signed under duress, really mattered.

Once our respective documents were approved we assumed

we could go. But Smoothy told us there was one more 'formality'. We were then taken into another basement room, where a television team was waiting – two cameramen and four interviewers, two male and two female. In the subsequent discussion, the women were more disagreeable than the men.

I started by saying that I refused to be interviewed, but the interrogators were present and they plainly indicated that we could not leave unless we talked. Margaret, in Russian, told them amiably what she had liked best on the tour and how well we had been received. Then I was asked to give my impressions. I said in English, that I intended to write about the journey and suggested my interviewers should read what I wrote. The woman who had asked the first question said that she looked forward to doing so, but why were the private addresses of Soviet citizens found listed in my notebooks? I replied that others wanted, as she did, to read my articles and I needed to know where to send them. The other woman asked how I could justify coming to their country as a guest and abusing my welcome by making hostile propaganda against the Soviet Union. As she was accusing me of a criminal offence, I replied that I found the question insulting. I neither wanted, nor was equipped, to make propaganda.

One of the men asked me about reports which had appeared 'in the Western press' alleging that British journalists were in the pay of the intelligence service. I said that I had heard the story (a damaging and unsubstantiated report which appeared in the *Washington Post*) and it was totally untrue. I had spent my life among Western journalists and had never met anyone who worked for an intelligence service. Later, I reflected that this was not strictly so. At *The Observer* I had once met Kim Philby during the period when he was working for the paper and certainly in the pay of Soviet intelligence. If my Soviet television interviewers read this book, they will accept my apology.

Had I during my journey seen any violation of human rights? 'I regard it as a violation of human rights that I have to appear before television cameras as a condition of being allowed to leave the country.' 'In view of the 20 million casualties the Soviet Union suffered during the last war, had I met anyone during my travels who wanted war?' 'No, I had not. Any more than I had met any war-wishers in the West.'

Then another question: 'A group of American tourists has recently visited our country and commented adversely on President Carter's foreign policy and the damage it is doing to détente. What is your opinion?' I looked at Smoothy and asked whether it was really necessary to conduct a discussion on international affairs before I could leave. 'No,' he said and the interview was over. Later British officials told me that Soviet TV was about to put on a British week in apparent retaliation for the BBC's 'Soviet Week' of the previous year, which had widely publicised the dissidents. Perhaps Margaret and I were supposed to be part of the show. In that case, our performance must have disappointed them. At my request, our Moscow Embassy monitored all the programmes and told me that we never appeared.

After our television performance a photographer took many 'stills' of me. I told him that if they came out well I would like copies. He laughed and took down my home address.

Before we left, Toughy said that he had a statement to make. He then read out a declaration from 'We, the representatives of the Soviet government', alleging that Margaret and I were both guilty of 'anti-Soviet agitation and propaganda'. Margaret was forgiven but I would not be allowed to return to the Soviet Union.

Yet as we left, Margaret was much more upset than I was: all her photographs were confiscated. Her husband had lent her his precious Praktika German camera and photography had taken up an enormous amount of her time and emotional energy. She had almost a hundred pictures to take back to him and had carefully avoided anything which could conceivably be considered 'strategic' – bridges, railways, airfields, ports. She had only taken scenery and people. Her husband had specially asked for slides he could use in his geography classes. Whenever we passed anything 'geographical', on went the brakes and out came the camera.

On the previous day, a soldier had told her that the pictures would be developed and the colour would disappear. He apologised that the frontier post only had the technical facilities for reproduction in black and white. But even black and white would have been better than none at all.

Both of us had already signed statements that we had no claims against the frontier officials. In my case the confiscation of two manuals and two newspapers was no material loss. Margaret reckoned that she had spent £25 on film. We were told to get into the car and they would bring us our passports. What about the photos? They would not be returned. Smoothy came to see us off and told Margaret she could come back and take as many pictures as she liked. There was one final hitch: we had to get out of the car again to sign a statement affirming that, while we were being searched, we had not been physically molested.

On the Hungarian side of the frontier the proceedings were swift. We reached the Hilton Hotel, Budapest by midnight. An embossed invitation to the Independence Party was handed to us at the desk. We were four hours too late.

Epilogue

The next morning I was so eager to register my protest that I arrived at our Embassy in Budapest at 9.30 a.m. and had to wait until the diplomats turned up. I reported that, on the Soviet side of the frontier, Margaret and I had been detained, accused of a criminal offence and refused access to the British Consul. The ambassador was sympathetic and cabled London immediately.

The day I got home, Mr Andrey Gromyko the Soviet Foreign Minister, in a speech reported in *The Times*, cited the Soviet Union as an example of a country which respects its international obligations. Two days later *The Times* published a letter from me saying that by now Mr Gromyko would have been told by his Embassy in London of the complaint made on my behalf by our Foreign Office. The Soviet Union, in refusing me access to our Consul, was in breach of an international convention. After briefly recounting what happened, I said 'I await Mr Gromyko's apologies.'

It was several weeks before the Soviet Embassy in London replied to the protest. When Mr Kenneth Scott, head of the Eastern-European and Soviet department of the Foreign Office, telephoned and gave me the official Soviet account of what had happened, I was so flabbergasted that I asked him to send it to me in writing.

Mr Scott's letter, dated 7 September 1978, recalled our telephone conversation and my request 'to have full details of the Soviet Embassy's reply' to the representations made on my behalf.

'As you know, after your call on me on the 7th of July I summoned a counsellor at the Soviet Embassy, a Mr Sokolov, later that day to make representations about the incident and to express the Government's concern about ιne evident contravention of the British–Soviet consular convention. We again raised the matter with Mr Sokolov on the 28th of July; he replied that the incident had been in reality a routine customs check, which had taken longer than usual because certain articles forbidden or restricted under Soviet customs regulations had been found on you. Mr Sokolov added that, as it was getting late in the day by the time the customs check had been completed, it had been suggested that you and Mrs Moss should spend the night in Chop and leave the next day; and that you had agreed. He said that there had been no question of any 'arrest', and that on leaving the USSR you had said that you had no complaints about the actions of the customs officials or about your treatment in Chop. Referring to your request to contact a lawyer from the British Embassy Mr Sikolov said you had been told this was not the practice during a customs check, and when the check had been completed you had not returned to the question.

'We pointed out to Mr Sokolov that his version differed in a number of important respects from your account of what had happened: for example, you had clearly told us that you had not been permitted to contact the British Embassy even from the hotel where you spent the night. We again asked for the return of the possessions confiscated from you and Mrs Moss.

'I reverted to the question and I saw another counsellor from the Soviet Embassy, Mr Kotliar, on 15th August. Mr Kotliar reiterated that you had not repeated your request to speak to the British Consul once the customs examination was over, and that you had offered and had accepted, the opportunity of spending the night in the hotel at Chop. He did not accept that you had done so because you had been told that you would be required for further questioning, or that you were denied permission to contact the Consul over night. I told Mr Kotliar that the Government were not satisfied with this explanation and asked

him to report back, but I have since heard no more.'
Neither Mr Scott nor I heard any more at all. I wrote to
Ambassador Lunkov, noting that the Soviet Government
regarded the incident as no more than a routine customs
check and saying that I therefore assumed there would be no
objection to my future visits to the Soviet Union.

Taken by itself, the frontier episode was little more than a
minor misadventure. It is not the normal treatment for motor
tourists in the Soviet Union. I was a writer. Any message from
Anatoli Kuznetsov was a red rag to the Soviet bull. And the
Russians were especially nervous about inquisitive Westerners,
knowing that hordes of them would be arriving for the 1980
Olympic Games.

What is significant is the startling contrast between the
events which took place during our twenty-four hours of
enforced detention at Chop and the official version of 'a
routine frontier check', given by the Soviet Embassy. For here,
in miniature, was a perfect illustration of the characteristic
divide between Soviet myth and Soviet reality. In no country,
at any time, has the contrast been so startling. It is worth
setting some of these side by side.

The image: a revolutionary society, breaking with the past.
The reality: an organism with inbuilt resistance to change and
a younger generation which looks to the West for anything
new and exciting.

The image: a country more peace-loving and dovish than
any in the world. The reality: little girls with ribbons in their
hair, goose-stepping with guns in front of war memorials. A
country, too, which indisputably spends a far higher
proportion of its resources and labour on its armed forces
than any Western power.

The image: a 'communist' or 'socialist' society with fair
shares and social equality. The reality, discovered by Orwell
thirty-five years ago: some are more equal than others. And
this is even truer now than in his day. Then, during the Stalin
terror, the potentates lived it up, but always at the risk of their
lives. Now there is stability and inherited privilege. Those at
the top of the pile can provide special education and special
jobs for their children. What does Gromyko junior know
about Africa, that he should qualify to be Director of the

Institute for African Affairs of the USSR Academy of Science? Very little, according to a Western diplomat, but he is the Foreign Minister's son.

The image: a country which champions national liberation movements. The reality: a sternly unitarian state which imposes Russian rule on nationally diverse populations, refuses to allow the Crimean Tartars to return from their wartime exile, and openly practises educational discrimination against the Jews.

The image: a workers' state. The reality, a system which bans strikes, imposes compulsory, unpaid overtime and, without restoring serfdom (abolished in Russia in 1861), still denies most peasants the internal passports required before they are allowed to leave the farm where they are employed. Many western workers still take this last claim seriously: Alex Kitson, executive officer of Britain's biggest trade union, the transport workers, is among the representatives of Western trade unions who have applauded the success of the Soviet 'worker state' in eliminating youthful unemployment. Britain and the United States could do likewise, at a stroke, by adopting the Soviet system of military conscription. Soviet men serve two or three years, depending on the region from which they come and the armed service to which they belong.

Tremendous resources and inventiveness are laid out by the Soviet Union in cultivating their image, and it has to be admitted that despite Solzhenitsyn, they have been astonishingly successful. But, when Western visitors and Soviet citizens mingle freely, there is a serious risk of the reality breaking through.

'Whatever do Soviet citizens have in common with foreign tourists?' The question was asked rhetorically by an anonymous writer of a letter published, with editorial support, in a Kharkov evening newspaper. The writer was denouncing his neighbour, who had received American visitors at his home. The proper answer is that Soviet citizens and foreign tourists have a lot in common and should really get to know each other better. Such a statement would be anathema to the Communist authorities but was plain common-sense to many of the people we met.

After all the talk of détente are the East and West any closer together? We should not take too seriously the official meetings, round tables and cultural exchanges inspired by the 1973 Helsinki Agreement. James Billington, head of the Wilson Institute, has pointed out that the Soviet Union carefully selects their participants, whereas the West lets anyone go. The consequence, he argues, is that Helsinki has helped Soviet Intelligence both to find out what they want to know and also to convey disinformation about what they want to conceal.

There is one way of establishing unofficial, uncensored contacts and that is to go in and meet the people. A motorist, travelling thousands of kilometres in his own car, cannot be watched all the time. You can police some of the people, some of the time, and we were often aware that we were being followed. But no country has a foolproof secret police.

For the Western visitor the journey is a pleasure as well as an eye-opener. Where the KGB and Party are involved, Soviet reality is worse than Soviet myth. But the peoples within the Soviet Union are more friendly, vibrant, open to change, than the monolithic apparatus and repetitive slogans suggest. In their splendid diversity, the southern regions of the USSR are well worth a visit and there is no better way of seeing places and meeting people than by private motor car. Travellers, go see for yourselves.

Index